Spanish
GCSE ROLE PLAYS
for AQA

higher
workbook

Ron Wallace
Series author: Jean-Claude Gilles

JOHN MURRAY

Also in this series:
French GCSE Role Plays for AQA Foundation Workbook   ISBN 0 7195 8143 5
(pack of 10)
French GCSE Role Plays for AQA Higher Workbook   ISBN 0 7195 8146 X
(pack of 10)
French GCSE Role Plays for AQA Audio on CD   ISBN 0 7195 8151 6
German GCSE Role Plays for AQA Foundation Workbook   ISBN 0 7195 8164 8
(pack of 10)
German GCSE Role Plays for AQA Higher Workbook   ISBN 0 7195 8165 6
(pack of 10)
German GCSE Role Plays for AQA Audio on CD   ISBN 0 7195 8161 3

AQA (NEAB)/AQA examination questions are reproduced by permission of the
Assessment and Qualifications Alliance.

First published 2003
by John Murray Publishers Ltd, a member of the Hodder Headline Group
338 Euston Road, London NW1 3BH

Cover design by John Townson/Creation
Typeset in 10/13pt Times Ten Roman by Fakenham Photosetting Ltd, Fakenham,
Norfolk NR21 8NN
Printed and bound in Great Britain by St Edmundsbury Press, Bury St Edmunds

A CIP catalogue record for this book is available from the British Library.

Foundation Workbook   ISBN 0 7195 8162 1 (pack of 10)
Higher Workbook   ISBN 0 7195 8163 X (pack of 10)
Audio on CD   ISBN 0 7195 8160 5

CONTENTS

INTRODUCTION

The role plays in this booklet have been adapted to meet the requirements of the GCSE Spanish Speaking Test and comply with the current AQA Specification (2003 onwards). The majority of them have been taken from recent past papers and amended to fit the new criteria.

■ FORMAT OF THE SPEAKING TEST

The Higher speaking test consists of **one** role play, followed by a presentation and discussion, and a general conversation. You are given ten minutes to prepare the role play under supervision and without dictionaries in the preparation room. You may make notes and read them out in the room where the test is conducted and recorded on tape by your own teacher. You can take as much or as little time as you like to go through the role play in the exam, but it is sensible to keep a steady pace and be aware of what your teacher is saying as you go along.

■ FORMAT OF THE ROLE PLAY

- The role play consists of four tasks for you to complete. The setting is given in English and your tasks are given in Spanish beside bullet points.
- One of the tasks has a large exclamation mark beside it. This means that you're not being given information about what you will hear, so you won't be able to prepare it and it's important to listen really carefully to what your teacher says in order to do the task.
- Your teacher will play the part of the other person in the role play and will start it off by speaking in Spanish. When your teacher stops speaking you should say what you have prepared for your first task.
- When you finish that, your teacher will speak again, and so on until you have completed all four tasks.
- If you stumble over your words, or slip up and correct yourself, try not to worry, but keep going. Your teacher will wait until you are ready to continue.
- If you can only do part of a task, just say what you have prepared. If it is appropriate and correct you may score something for what you have said.
- If you can't do one of the tasks at all, just tell your teacher, who will go on to introduce the next task for you. You could say something like *No sé* (I don't know) or *No entiendo* (I don't understand).

■ THE MARK SCHEME

There are up to **four** marks available for each task, so the maximum you can score is **16** marks. No half marks are awarded. The assessment of each task is based on the communication of the message and the quality of the language, and is as follows:

Criteria for assessment
Higher role play – Communication and quality of language

0 marks   Required message not communicated

1 mark   Appropriate response, although inaccuracy or loss of part of the message may cause difficulty of ambiguity for comprehension. The task may not be fully accomplished, but some relevant information is communicated.

2 marks   Appropriate and unambiguous response, although there may be minor errors or omission of a minor element of the message

3 marks   Appropriate and full response. Quality of language is such that minor errors would cause no difficulties of comprehension.

4 marks   Appropriate and correct response. The task is accomplished fully and without significant error*.

*without significant error – grammatically correct but may contain one minor error. If an answer contains more than one minor error, 3 marks maximum may be awarded.

The mark schemes in this workbook have been written by the author based on the structure and principles of the AQA GCSE Higher mark schemes, but with some clarification for teachers' ease of reference, and to reflect the most recent practice in the marking of role-play examinations by AQA. These mark schemes have been reviewed and approved by AQA.

■ THE FEATURES OF THE BOOKLET
- The candidate tasks are printed on the right-hand page; underneath the tasks there is some helpful advice to help you if you are stuck, and space for you to make notes for your answers.
- The teacher/examiner's prompts are printed on the back of the candidate's page, with a detailed mark scheme showing a range of scoring and non-scoring answers.
- At the back of the booklet there is an English–Spanish word list that contains some of the key vocabulary you may need.
- There is also a CD to accompany the booklet; for each role play it contains the examiner's role, and an example of a good performance by a potential A-grade candidate.

Using the booklet on your own
The role plays are arranged by theme; 1–3 fall under the topic 'My World', 4–14 under 'Holiday time and travel', 15–23 under 'Work and lifestyle', and 24–30 under 'The young person in society'. However, you can practise them in any order. You may find it useful to choose one that is relevant to a topic you have just done in class, or you may prefer to use it for revision purposes nearer the exam time. To give yourself the chance to experience the test as realistically as possible, prepare the tasks without help from your own notes or the vocabulary, and don't spend longer than ten minutes on it. You may indeed do it more quickly. When you have written down your answers turn over the page and check them against the mark scheme. If you don't see your particular answers there, then consult your teacher.

Using the booklet with a partner
If you work with somebody else, you can take it in turns to be the teacher and the candidate. Spend up to ten minutes preparing what to say (including writing out what you want to say) then act out the role play in full, so that each of you gets the feel of what it's like to be the candidate and the teacher. When you've completed it you can check your answers together using the mark scheme, and discuss what was easy or difficult.

Recording the role play on tape
It can be a very useful exercise to record what you say, either on your own or with a partner. Listening to it afterwards will let you hear how

clear it sounds and how well you've pronounced individual words and whole phrases. Ask yourself if it's loud enough. Did you speak clearly, or too fast or too slowly? What was your pronunciation like, in terms of individual letters and complete words? What about your intonation? Did a question sound like a question, for example? Think what you need to do to improve it. Have another go at it and see if that sounds better. Ask someone else to comment on it, like your teacher. Finally, have a listen to the model role plays on the accompanying CD and see how your performance compares!

■ TOP TIPS FOR SPANISH ROLE PLAYS

Although the role plays change year after year, there are many similar tasks in them. They also contain many key phrases, words and verbs that appear in different settings. This section gives you a summary of some of the most important things to remember and look out for before you do your role play.

Essential verbs for Spanish role plays

Here is a list of some of the more common verbs that you will need in Spanish role-play tasks.

1 am / are (permanent characteristics)   *ser*
I'm English.   *Soy inglés/inglesa.*

2 am / are (+ profession)   *ser*
I'm a waiter/waitress.   *Soy camarero/a.*

3 am / are (temporary characteristics)   *estar*
I'm tired.   *Estoy cansado/a.*

4 am (various uses)   *ser / estar / tener*
I'm on holiday. (temporary)   *Estoy de vacaciones.*
I'm fifteen years old. (age)   *Tengo quince años.*
I'm hungry and thirsty.   *Tengo hambre y sed.*

5 can / can't   *poder*
I can (can't) go on Saturday.   *(No) puedo ir el sábado.*

6 could (conditional tense)   *poder*
We could play tennis.   *Podríamos jugar al tenis.*

7 don't / doesn't / didn't (auxiliary verb)
I don't want to go to the cinema.   *No quiero ir al cine.*
He doesn't speak English.   *No habla inglés.*
I didn't reserve a room.   *No reservé una habitación.*

8 go   *ir*
I go to school by bus.   *Voy al instituto en autobús.*
I am going to the beach.   *Voy a la playa.*

9 have (got)   *tener*
I have a problem.   *Tengo un problema.*

10 have (+ past participle)   *haber*
I've lost my suitcase.   *He perdido mi maleta.*

11 have to / must   *tener que*
I have to go home tomorrow.   *Tengo que volver a casa mañana.*
I must telephone my parents.   *Tengo que llamar a mis padres.*

12 is / are (permanent characteristics)   *ser*
The waiter is tall and blond.   *El camarero es alto y rubio.*

13 is / are (temporary characteristics)   *estar*
The disco is closed.   *La discoteca está cerrada.*

14 is / are (position, location)   *estar*
My friend is in his room.   *Mi amigo está en su dormitorio.*

15 is (weather)
It is very hot in August.

hacer
Hace mucho calor en agosto.

16 leave
I left my bag on the bus.
The bus left at eight o clock.

dejar / salir de . . .
Dejé mi bolsa en el autobús.
El autobús salió a las ocho.

17 let's . . .
Let's go to the beach tomorrow.

vamos a . . .
Vamos a la playa mañana.

18 like / prefer
I like going to the beach.
I prefer blue.

gustar / preferir
Me gusta ir a la playa.
Prefiero el azul.

19 there is / there are
There is a good film on TV.
There are no towels in my room.

hay
Hay una buena película en la televisión.
No hay toallas en mi habitación.

20 want
I want to play tennis.

querer
Quiero jugar al tenis.

21 went
I went to the sports centre.
He/she went to the sports centre.

ir
Fui al polideportivo.
Fue al polideportivo.

22 work
I work in a shop.
The shower doesn't work.

trabajar / funcionar
Trabajo en una tienda.
La ducha no funciona.

23 would like
I would like to go to the beach.

gustar
Me gustaría ir a la playa.

Question words for Spanish role plays

At Higher tier the teacher's script contains a lot of questions or phrases requesting information, so it's important to listen to them carefully, particularly when you get to the unpredictable task, where it will be crucial. Use this list for reference.

1 ¿a qué hora?
¿A qué hora llegó el avión?

what time . . .?
What time did the plane arrive?

2 ¿adónde?
¿Adónde fuiste el año pasado?

where to?
Where did you go last year?

3 ¿cómo?
¿Cómo vas al instituto?
¿Cómo se escribe su apellido?
¿Cómo va a pagar?
¿Cómo sería tu trabajo ideal?

how / what . . . like?
How do you go to school?
How do you spell your surname?
How are you going to pay?
What would your ideal job be like?

4 ¿cómo? / ¿qué tal?
¿Cómo estás?
¿Qué tal la excursión?

how is / are / was . . . ?
How are you?
How was the excursion?

5 ¿cómo se llama . . .?
¿Cómo se llama tu personaje favorito?

what . . . name / called?
What's your favourite character called?

6 ¿cuál? / ¿cuáles?
¿Cuál prefieres?
¿Cuál es el problema exactamente?
¿Cuál es tu opinión sobre . . .?
¿Cuáles son las ventajas de . . .?

which (of a choice)? / what?
Which one do you prefer?
What exactly is the problem?
What's your opinion about . . .?
What are the advantages of . . .?

7 ¿cuándo?
¿Cuándo ocurrió el accidente?

when?
When did the accident happen?

8 ¿cuánto?
¿Cuántas habitaciones necesita usted?
¿Cuánto tiempo vas a quedarte?

how much / many?
How many rooms do you need?
How long are you going to stay?

9 ¿cuántos años . . .?

how old . . .?

¿Cuántos años tiene usted?	How old are you?
10 deme / explíqueme	**give me some details ...**
Deme unos detalles del vuelo.	Give me details about the flight.
11 descríbame / descríbeme	**describe ...**
Descríbame su camarero, por favor.	Describe your waiter, please.
12 ¿dónde?	**where?**
¿Dónde ocurrió el accidente?	Where did the accident happen?
13 háblame / hábleme	**tell me ...**
Háblame un poco de tu región.	Tell me a bit about your area.
14 ¿por qué? / porque ...	**why? / because ...**
¿Por qué te gusta el programa?	Why do you like the programme?
Porque es muy divertido.	Because it's very entertaining.
¿Por qué dices eso?	Why do you say that?
15 ¿qué?	**what?**
¿Qué piensas hacer el año que viene?	What are you planning to do next year?
¿Qué (otra cosa) podemos hacer?	What (else) can we do?
¿Qué más puede usted decirme?	What else can you tell me?
¿De qué trata la película?	What's the film about?
16 ¿quién?	**who?**
¿Quién conducía el coche?	Who was driving the car?

Accuracy in Spanish role plays

Higher role plays are marked on communication and quality of language. To score full marks for a task (4 out of 4) you need to communicate the message fully (which means you mustn't leave anything important out), and you are allowed **one minor error** (for example a wrong gender of a noun, or an incorrect agreement of an adjective). As soon as you make **two minor errors**, but still communicate the message fully, the mark awarded drops to 3 out of 4. If you make **three or more minor errors** but communicate the whole message the mark drops to 2 out of 4. A **major error** (for example the wrong person of a verb, or an incorrect tense) is likely to affect communication seriously and the mark could go down to 1 or 0 out of 4. A **minor omission** of part of a task, even before taking the accuracy into account, will mean that the maximum you can be awarded is 2 out of 4. If you study the mark scheme closely, you will see that verbs are an important part of each task, so if you respond without verbs, you are unlikely to score more than 2 out of 4. Occasionally infinitives are acceptable, but more often than not you will need to use an appropriate tense and person of each verb. Your pronunciation is important in this, too. If you don't make your verb ending clear, the examiner may not be able to award marks. Simple examples would be *se llamo* (where the final 'o' should be an 'a'), or *fue* (for *fui* when you need to say 'I went').

Pronunciation tips for Spanish role plays

- Remember the difference between a hard 'c' and a soft 'c', or between 'r' and 'rr'. Try pronouncing the words **cin**co and **cer**ca, or pe**r**o and pe**rr**o, for example.
- Some letters aren't pronounced at all, of course. The **h** is a good example, but also beware of the letter **u** in a word like *pequeño*, which is pronounced '*pe-ke-nyo*' rather than '*pe-kwe-nyo*'. Poor pronunciation of this could lose you marks.
- The double *ll* can sometimes cause a problem, too. A good example is *toalla*, the Spanish word for 'towel', which is pronounced 'toal-ya'. Practise saying these ones as well: *me llamo* = 'me lyamo' (my name is ...); *llueve* = 'lyu-ebe' (it rains/is raining); and the Spanish dish *paella*, 'pa-el-ya'.

ROLE PLAY 1

CANDIDATE'S ROLE

> You are in Spain. You telephone your Spanish friend and invite him/her to go to a disco in Torremolinos on Saturday night.
>
> **a)**   • *Tu sugerencia – dónde y cuándo*.
> **b)**   • **Dos** *opiniones de la discoteca*.
> **c)**   • **Dos** *actividades diferentes*.
> **d)**   • !
>
> When you see ! you will have to respond to something which you have not prepared. Your teacher will play the part of your friend and will speak first.

■ TO HELP YOU

a) Use the rubric to help you work out the first task. Here it means you say the Spanish equivalent of 'Do you want to go to a disco on Saturday night?' You need two verbs: 'want' and 'go'. The first one, *querer*, is irregular (it's actually 'radical changing') and you need the second person singular. The second verb should stay in the infinitive. Be careful – the common word for 'on' is not *en* for days of the week! Say 'the Saturday' then add the phrase 'by night'. Remember to make your voice rise when you say the question!

b) There are no right or wrong opinions, but try to keep your language simple and accurate. How about: 'the music is very good' or 'there are lots of young people' or 'the atmosphere is excellent'?

c) The implication here is that you need to suggest two different things to do. Perhaps your Spanish friend doesn't like discos! Maybe you could say: 'We can go to the cinema or watch television', or something like that. 'We can' comes from *poder*, and the other verbs will be infinitives.

d) This is the unpredictable task! If the previous task asks you to suggest **two** activities to your friend, what might he/she ask next? Always be prepared to justify your answer.

■ JOT DOWN YOUR ANSWERS

a) _____

b) _____

c) _____

d) _____

TEACHER'S ROLE

1 Introduce the situation and then answer the telephone.
Estás hablando con tu amigo español/tu amiga española. Yo soy tu amigo/amiga.
¡Dígame!

2 Allow the candidate to invite you to a disco in Torremolinos on Saturday night.
Ask why he/she wants to go. Elicit **two** reasons.
¿Por qué quieres ir allí?

3 Allow the candidate to give **two** reasons for going to the disco.
Say that you do not like discos much, and ask what else you could do. Elicit **two** activities.
No me gustan mucho las discotecas. ¿Qué otras actividades recomiendas?

4 **!** Allow the candidate to suggest **two** other activities.
Ask the candidate which he/she prefers and why. Elicit **two** reasons.
¿Cuál prefieres tú? . . . ¿Por qué?

5 Allow the candidate to say which he/she prefers and to give **two** reasons why.
End the conversation by agreeing with the suggestion.
De acuerdo. Hasta luego.

■ MARK SCHEME

	0	1	2	3	4
	Message not communicated	Appropriate response/ difficulty or ambiguity/ some relevant information	Appropriate and unambiguous/minor errors or minor omissions	Appropriate and full response/minor errors cause no ambiguity/ TWO minor errors max.	Appropriate and correct response/task fully accomplished/NO SIGNIFICANT ERROR/ ONE minor error max.
a)	Wrong person of verb	*¿Quieres va . . .?*	Omission of *sábado* + rest correct	Two minor errors, e.g. *¿Quieres ir discoteca sábado?*	*¿Quieres ir a la discoteca (en Torremolinos) el sábado (por la noche)?*
b)		**One** detail only	Two opinions, no verb e.g. *música buena; muchos jóvenes*	Two minor errors, e.g. *el música es buena; hay muchos jóvens*	**Two** opinions with verb(s) essential, e.g. *la música es muy buena; hay muchos jóvenes*
c)		**One** activity only with or without verb	Two activities, no verb *Voy a ir a . . . +* two places	Two minor errors, e.g. *ir cine, ver televisión*	Verb(s) essential, e.g. *(podemos) ir al cine (o) ver la televisión*
d)		**One** reason only Response alone, e.g. *cine* (on its own)		Two minor errors	**Two** reasons essential e.g. *(prefiero el) cine (porque) es divertido y ponen una película muy buena*

CANDIDATE'S ROLE

> You are staying with your Spanish friend. He/She is keen to know more about where you are from.
>
> **a)**   • *Tres detalles de tu región – situación y descripción.*
> **b)**   • *Tres detalles del clima.*
> **c)**   • *Una actividad favorita de los jóvenes, y razón.*
> **d)**   • !
>
> When you see ! you will have to respond to something which you have not prepared. Your teacher will play the part of your friend and will speak first.

■ TO HELP YOU

a) Name your region (if you want) and say where it is (e.g. in the north/south; by the sea; etc.). Then describe it by saying, for example, 'it is … (+ adjectives)' or 'there are … (+ nouns)'. Remember that there are two verbs for 'to be' in Spanish: *estar* (for position or location) and *ser* (for permanent characteristics). Use them correctly, and make sure you give **three** details altogether!

b) What's the weather like in your area? Pretty varied, perhaps? Give **three** examples of fairly common weather conditions, and make sure you use the correct verb(s): do you need *hacer*, *estar*, or a completely separate verb? Try not to add too much extra language unless you're very sure it's right!

c) Choose any **one** activity that's popular with young people in your area (e.g. sport, free time interest, shopping, etc.). You can use a verb in the infinitive (and add something like '… is a favourite activity' if you want) but it's important to give a reason. Use the word for 'because' (if you want) and keep the reason simple: 'it's + adjective', for example.

d) This is the unpredictable task! The theme of this role play is 'the areas people live in'. What might your friend go on to ask? Always be prepared to give reasons for your answer.

■ JOT DOWN YOUR ANSWERS

a) _____

b) _____

c) _____

d) _____

TEACHER'S ROLE

1 Explain the situation and ask the candidate to tell you about the area he/she lives in. Elicit **three** details, including where it is.
Estás hablando de tu región con tu amigo español/tu amiga española. Yo soy tu amigo/amiga.
Háblame un poco de tu región.

2 Allow the candidate to offer **three** details about the area he/she lives in.
Ask him/her what the weather is like there. Elicit **three** details about the weather.
Y ¿cómo es el clima?

3 Allow the candidate to give **three** details about the weather.
Ask him/her what the favourite activity is for young people in the area, and why.

Bueno, ¿cuál es la actividad favorita de los jóvenes allí? . . . ¿Por qué?

4 ❗ Allow the candidate to mention the favourite activity of young people and give a reason for it. Ask if he/she would like to live elsewhere in his/her country and why/why not. Elicit **two** reasons.
¿Te gustaría vivir en otra parte de tu país? . . . ¿Por qué (no)?

5 Allow the candidate to give **two** reasons why he/she would or would not like to live elsewhere in his/her country.
End the conversation by saying you do not want to live anywhere else in Spain.
Pues yo no quiero vivir en otra parte de España.

■ MARK SCHEME

	0	1	2	3	4
	Message not communicated	Appropriate response/ difficulty or ambiguity/ some relevant information	Appropriate and unambiguous/minor errors or minor omissions	Appropriate and full response/minor errors cause no ambiguity/ TWO minor errors max.	Appropriate and correct response/task fully accomplished/NO SIGNIFICANT ERROR/ ONE minor error max.
a)	Name of region only	**One** detail only (with verb) **Two** details (one situation + one description) **without** verbs e.g. *en el norte;* and *industrial.*	**Three** details **without** verb(s) **Two** details (must be one situation + one description) **with** verbs	All **three** details with **verb(s)**, e.g. *Kent está en sureste de Inglaterra. Es mucho bonito y tranquilo.*	**Three** clear details (at least one situation and one description) **with** verb(s) e.g. *Kent está en el sureste de Inglaterra. Es bonito y tranquilo.*
b)		**One** detail only	**Two** details without errors. No need for verb(s) here if message is clear, e.g. *Frío y viento.*	All **three** details **with** verb(s) with minor errors, e.g. *Hace muy frío y viento. Llueve no mucho.*	**Three** clear details of climate with verb(s), e.g. *Hace mucho frío y viento. No llueve mucho.*
c)		**One** element only, e.g. *bolera* (on its own)	Activity + reason conveyed however basically, **without** verb(s), e.g. *bolera (porque) divertido.*	Activity + reason **with** verb(s), e.g. *Ir bolera (porque) es mucho divertido.*	One clear activity with appropriate reason **with** verb(s), e.g. *Ir a la bolera (es una actividad favorita) (porque) es muy divertido.*
d)		*Sí* or *No* plus some ambiguity *Sí* or *No* (on its own)	*Sí* or *No* OK plus **one** reason, **with** verb(s) *Sí* or *No* OK plus **two** reasons, **without** verb(s)	*Sí* or *No* plus **two** reasons **with** verb(s), e.g. *No, tengo mucho amigos (y) hay mucho hacer.*	*Sí* or *No* OK plus **two** reasons, **with** verb(s), e.g. *No, (porque) tengo muchos amigos (aquí) (y) hay mucho que hacer.*

CANDIDATE'S ROLE

> You have just spent the day in a school in Spain with your Spanish friend.
>
> a) • ***Dos*** *diferencias entre tu instituto y el instituto español.*
> b) • *Tus estudios de español – cuánto tiempo; otros idiomas.*
> c) • *Planes para septiembre y tu razón.*
> d) • !
>
> When you see ! you will have to respond to something which you have not prepared. Your teacher will play the part of your friend and will speak first.

■ TO HELP YOU

a) You might consider differences such as timetable, subjects, start and finish times, uniform, lunch, holidays, rules or homework, for example. Keep your **two** statements fairly simple and do refer to either your school or a Spanish one in order to show the 'difference' or make a comparison.

b) Say how many years you've been studying Spanish for, and remember that you need the first person singular of the present tense of the verb 'study' together with the special word 'for'. Is it *para*, *desde* or *desde hace* that you need? Remember to say if you study another foreign language (or not), too!

c) Either the future or the near future tense could help you to say what you plan to do in September. Consider things like study (certain subjects) or work (as a . . .). Use simple Spanish and try to avoid difficult phrases such as 'be in the Sixth Form', for example. Remember to give a sensible reason for your plans.

d) This is the unpredictable task! The theme of this role play is 'school and future plans'. What else might your friend go on to ask? Always be prepared to give more than one detail in your answer. If your teacher thinks you haven't given enough information he/she might encourage you to add something else by asking *¿Algo más?*

■ JOT DOWN YOUR ANSWERS

a) _____

b) _____

c) _____

d) _____

ROLE PLAY 3
TEACHER'S ROLE

1 Explain the situation and then ask the candidate what differences he/she has noticed between his/her school and the Spanish one. Elicit **two** differences.
Estás hablando del instituto con tu amigo español/tu amiga española. Yo soy tu amigo/amiga.
¿Qué diferencias has notado entre tu instituto y el mío?

2 Allow the candidate to give **two** differences between his/her school and the Spanish one.
Ask how long he/she has been studying Spanish and whether he/she studies any other languages.
Y ¿hace cuánto tiempo que estudias español? . . . ¿Estudias otros idiomas?

3 Allow the candidate to say how long he/she has been studying Spanish and whether he/she studies any other languages.

Ask him/her what he/she intends to do in September, and why.
¿Qué piensas hacer en septiembre? . . . ¿Por qué?

4 🖁 Allow the candidate to say what he/she intends to do in September and why.
Ask the candidate what plans he/she has for the holidays before September. Elicit **two** details.
Y antes de septiembre, ¿qué planes tienes para las vacaciones?

5 Allow the candidate to give **two** details about the plans he/she has for the holidays before September. End the conversation by saying that you hope he/she has a good time.
Bueno, que lo pases bien.

■ MARK SCHEME

	0	1	2	3	4
	Message not communicated	Appropriate response/ difficulty or ambiguity/ some relevant information	Appropriate and unambiguous/minor errors or minor omissions	Appropriate and full response/minor errors cause no ambiguity/ TWO minor errors max.	Appropriate and correct response/task fully accomplished/NO SIGNIFICANT ERROR/ ONE minor error max.
a)		**One** difference only	**Two** differences **without** verbs	**Two** differences **with** verbs, e.g. *Hay no uniforme (y) el día es más larga (en tu colegio).*	**Two** differences **with** verbs, e.g. *No hay uniforme (y) el día es más largo (en tu colegio).*
b)	Number on its own	**One** element only	Appropriate response **without** verbs Two elements however basic, e.g. *español tres años y francés.*	**Both** elements conveyed **with** verbs, e.g. *Estudio español desde tres años. (También) estudios francés.*	**Both** elements conveyed **with** verbs, e.g. *Estudio español desde hace tres años. (También) estudio francés.*
c)		Response only	Response + reason **without** a verb Lack of verb in opinion (e.g. *dinero* on its own)	Response + reason **with** verb(s), e.g. *Voy buscar trabajo (porque) quiero el dinero.* (with incorrect pronunciation of 'j' or 'kwiero')	Response + reason **with** verb(s), e.g. *(Voy a buscar) trabajo (porque) quiero el dinero.*
d)	No relevant information conveyed, e.g. *vacaciones* on its own	**One** detail only however basic	**Two** details without verb(s) (e.g. *discoteca y trabajo*)	**Two** details **with** verb(s), e.g. *ir la playa (y) viajar* (with incorrect pronunciation of 'j')	**Two** clear details with verb(s) Verb alone may include activity e.g. *ir a la playa (y) viajar.*

CANDIDATE'S ROLE

> You are on holiday in Alicante in Spain. You want to go to Valencia for the weekend. **You must be back in Alicante on Sunday evening**. You go to the Tourist Office to make travel arrangements.
>
> **a)** • *Detalles del viaje planeado – adónde y cuándo.*
> **b)** • *Transporte preferido y tu razón.*
> **c)** •
> **d)** • ***Dos** opiniones de tus vacaciones en España.*
>
> When you see you will have to respond to something which you have not prepared. Your teacher will play the part of the Tourist Office employee and will speak first.

■ TO HELP YOU

a) You need to say where and when you want to go. There are two places mentioned so make sure you say the right one! To say 'I want ...' or 'I would like ...' use the verb *querer* (present tense, or special form of the conditional) or *gustar* (conditional tense). It will be followed by the infinitive 'to go'. Also remember to say 'at the', or 'for the', or 'this' weekend.

b) The verb *preferir* is a 'radical changing' verb that's extremely useful to know. You will need the first person singular, but be very careful to pronounce all the vowels in the right order! Choose any method of transport you want. Remember to give a simple reason for your choice.

c) This is the unpredictable task! But notice the rubric in bold type at the beginning of the role play. This will give you a big clue! Could it be that the Tourist Office employee might put an obstacle in your way? Be ready to give him/her this information. (Remember that 'must' is the same as 'have to' and 'be back' is the same as 'return'.)

d) Here is an opportunity to give two opinions about your holiday in Spain. You could comment on the country, the region, the people, your accommodation, the things to do, the weather, the food, etc. The list is almost endless!

■ JOT DOWN YOUR ANSWERS

a) _____

b) _____

c) _____

d) _____

TEACHER'S ROLE

1 Begin the conversation by explaining the situation and then greet the candidate and ask how you can help him/her.
Estamos en la oficina de turismo de Alicante. Yo soy el empleado/la empleada. ¡Hola! Buenos días. ¿En qué puedo ayudarle?

2 Allow the candidate to give details of where and when he/she wishes to travel. Ask for more information about his/her journey and elicit a reason for his/her preference of transport chosen.
Muy bien. ¿Qué más puede usted decirme sobre el viaje? . . . ¿Por qué?

3 ❗ Allow the candidate to give you more information about his/her journey and the reason for his/her preference.
Tell him/her it will not be possible to return on Sunday as there is a fiesta. Say he/she will have to return on Monday morning. Ask if that is OK, and when he/she says not, ask why.

Pues el domingo es la fiesta mayor y no hay transportes. Tendrá que volver el lunes por la mañana. ¿Está bien? . . . ¿Por qué no?

4 Allow the candidate to say that it will not be possible for him/her to return on Monday morning and to say why.
Suggest that he/she goes to another place, such as Benidorm. Finally, ask if he/she has liked his/her holidays in Spain and why/why not. Elicit **two** reasons.
Entonces mejor ir a otro sitio, como Benidorm. ¿Le han gustado sus vacaciones en España? . . . ¿Por qué/por qué no?

5 Allow the candidate to say if he/she has liked his/her holidays in Spain, and to give **two** reasons why/why not.
End the conversation by saying that's interesting.
¡Qué interesante!

■ MARK SCHEME

	0	1	2	3	4
	Message not communicated	Appropriate response/ difficulty or ambiguity/ some relevant information	Appropriate and unambiguous/minor errors or minor omissions	Appropriate and full response/minor errors cause no ambiguity/ TWO minor errors max.	Appropriate and correct response/task fully accomplished/NO SIGNIFICANT ERROR/ ONE minor error max.
a)	Wrong place and/or day(s)	Wrong tense *Ir Valencia* (on its own)	Appropriate response **without** verb(s), e.g. *Valencia fin de semana.*	Place and time **with** verb(s), e.g. *Quiero ir Valencia este fin de semana.*	Where and when stated **with** verb(s), e.g. *ir a Quiero Valencia este/el fin de semana.*
b)	Reason only	Choice of transport only, e.g. *tren* (on its own)	Appropriate response even if no verb(s), e.g. *Tren (porque) . . . (muy) rápido.*	Transport + reason **with** verb(s), e.g. *Prefiero ir el tren (porque) es (muy) rápido.* (with incorrect pronunciation of 'preferio')	Clear choice of transport + reason **with** verb(s), e.g. *Prefiero (ir en) (el) tren (porque) es (muy) rápido.*
c)	*Sí.* (a positive response)	*No.* (Response on its own)	*No* + reason **without** verbs, e.g. *(porque) yo aquí Alicante domingo noche.*	*No* plus reason **with** verb(s), e.g. *No, (porque) tengo que volver Alicante el domingo noche.*	*No* plus reason **with** verb(s), e.g. *(porque) tengo que volver a Alicante el domingo por la noche.*
d)		Response only One reason only	All elements clearly conveyed **without** verb(s), e.g. *(porque región bonita (y) mucho sol.*	Response plus **two** reasons **with** verb(s), e.g. *(porque) el región es bonita (y) hace muy sol.*	*Sí/No* plus **two** reasons **with** verb(s), e.g. *(porque) la región es bonita (y) hace mucho sol.*

CANDIDATE'S ROLE

You are on holiday in Spain. You have just got on a train to Barcelona and cannot find a seat in second class. You ask a guard on the train to help you.

a) • *Tu problema.*

b) • *Tu razón por no reservar un asiento.*

c) • *Tu solución para resolver el problema.*

d) • ❗

When you see ❗ you will have to respond to something which you have not prepared. Your teacher will play the part of the guard and will speak first.

■ TO HELP YOU

a) Use the rubric to help you work out the first task. Here it means you say the Spanish equivalent of 'I cannot find a seat in second class'. Use the first person singular of the radical changing verb *poder* followed by the infinitive of the verb 'find'. The rest is fairly straightforward, and remember the *no* at the beginning!

b) You only have to give one reason why you didn't reserve a seat. Maybe you didn't have time this morning, or you arrived late at the station, or there were a lot of people in the ticket office ... Whatever you say make sure you use a past tense, probably a preterite (I didn't have time .../I arrived late ...) or an imperfect (there were ...).

c) So how do you want to solve this problem? Perhaps you want a seat in first class, or you want a refund, or you want a free drink in the restaurant car, or you want to get the next train. All of these options will need the first person singular of the radical changing verb *querer*.

d) This is the unpredictable task! The only other information that might be useful to you in the rubric is perhaps your destination, Barcelona. What might the guard ask you?

■ JOT DOWN YOUR ANSWERS

a) _____

b) _____

c) _____

d) _____

TEACHER'S ROLE

1 Introduce the situation, then ask the candidate how you can help.
Estamos en un tren. Yo soy el revisor/la revisora.
¿En qué puedo ayudarle, señor/señora/señorita?

2 Allow the candidate to say he/she cannot find a seat in second class.
Sympathise and ask why the candidate did not reserve a seat.
Lo siento. ¿Por qué no reservó usted un asiento en el tren?

3 Allow the candidate to say why he/she did not reserve a seat.
Ask the candidate what he/she wants to do.
¿Qué quiere hacer para resolver el problema?

4 ❗ Allow the candidate to suggest a solution.
Agree with the candidate's solution. Ask the candidate about his/her plans for the holidays in Barcelona. Elicit **two** details.
Muy bien. ¿Qué planes tiene usted para sus vacaciones en Barcelona?

5 Allow the candidate to give **two** details of his/her plans for the holidays in Barcelona.
End the conversation by wishing the candidate a happy holiday.
Muy bien. ¡Buenas vacaciones!

■ MARK SCHEME

	0	1	2	3	4
	Message not communicated	Appropriate response/ difficulty or ambiguity/ some relevant information	Appropriate and unambiguous/minor errors or minor omissions	Appropriate and full response/minor errors cause no ambiguity/ TWO minor errors max.	Appropriate and correct response/task fully accomplished/NO SIGNIFICANT ERROR/ ONE minor error max.
a)	Inappropriate response *Segunda clase* (on its own)	Appropriate response – one element only, e.g. *No hay asiento.*	Appropriate response without verb, e.g. *No asiento en segunda clase.*	Explanation **with** verb(s), e.g. *No encontrar (un) segunda clase asiento.*	Clear explanation of the problem; verb essential, e.g. *No puedo encontrar (un) asiento en segunda clase.*
b)		Ambiguous response, e.g. *Tiempo* (on its own)	Appropriate response **without** verb(s), e.g. *No tiempo por la mañana.*	Appropriate response **with** verb(s), e.g. *No tener tiempo en mañana.*	Appropriate response **with** verb(s), e.g. *No tuve tiempo esta mañana.*
c)		Ambiguous response, e.g. *Primera clase* (on its own)	Appropriate response **without** verb(s), e.g. *¿Asiento en primera clase?*	Appropriate response **with** verb(s), e.g. *Quiero un asiento en primero clase.* (with incorrect pronunciation 'kwiero')	Appropriate response **with** verb(s), e.g. *Quiero un asiento en primera clase.*
d)		**One** detail only, e.g. *Ver la catedral.*	**Two** details but **without** verbs, e.g. *el museo y la catedral.*	**Two** details **with** verb(s), e.g. *Voy un museo y (ver) el catedral.*	**Two** clear details of plans **with** verb(s), e.g. *Voy a (visitar) un museo y (ver) la catedral.*

ROLE PLAY 6

CANDIDATE'S ROLE

> You have just arrived at a Spanish airport. When you go to collect your suitcase you find it has not arrived. You go to the information desk where you speak to the receptionist.
>
> **a)**   • *Tu problema.*
> **b)**   • ***Dos*** *detalles de tu vuelo.*
> **c)**   • █!█
> **d)**   • *Tus planes para el día (**dos** detalles).*
>
> When you see █!█ you will have to respond to something which you have not prepared. Your teacher will play the part of the receptionist and will speak first.

■ TO HELP YOU

a) Use the rubric to help you work out the first task. Simply tell the receptionist 'My suitcase has not arrived'. You'll need a past tense, either the perfect or the preterite. Be careful about the word order if you use the perfect tense. Where will you put the word *no*? And what verb do you need for the auxiliary verb 'have' in the perfect tense – *tener*, *haber* or *tomar*?

b) You need to give the receptionist **two** details about your flight, for example: its number, where you arrived from, the time you left, the time you arrived, etc. Perhaps you could make two separate statements, each one with a verb: 'it is flight number . . . from . . .' and 'I/it arrived at . . .'.

c) This is the unpredictable task! What will it be important for the receptionist to know if he/she is going to be able to find your suitcase? How much detail can you supply? (Remember there are four marks available for the task!)

d) The question *¿Qué planes tiene(s)?* usually indicates a time in the future. If the receptionist is to contact you this afternoon it's logical for you to say what you're going to be doing (*voy a . . .* + infinitive; or simple future tense). You need to give **two** details, so that could be an activity and a place, for example.

■ JOT DOWN YOUR ANSWERS

a) _____

b) _____

c) _____

d) _____

ROLE PLAY 6

TEACHER'S ROLE

1 Introduce the situation, then ask what the problem is.
Estamos en un aeropuerto en España. Yo soy un/una recepcionista.
¿Cuál es su problema, señor/señora/señorita?

2 Allow the candidate to say his/her suitcase has not arrived.
Ask the candidate for his/her flight details. Elicit **two** details.
Explíqueme los detalles de su vuelo, por favor.

3 ⚠ Allow the candidate to give **two** details about his/her flight.
Ask the candidate to describe his/her suitcase and its contents. Elicit **two** details about the case and **two** details about its contents.
Descríbame su maleta. . . . Y ¿dentro de la maleta?

4 Allow the candidate to give **two** details about the case and **two** details about its contents.
Ask what plans the candidate has for the rest of the day. Elicit **two** details.
¿Qué planes tiene usted para el resto del día?

5 Allow the candidate to give **two** details about his/her plans for the rest of the day.
End the conversation by saying you will send the suitcase to the candidate as soon as it arrives.
Entonces le mandaremos su maleta en cuanto llegue.

■ MARK SCHEME

	0	1	2	3	4
	Message not communicated	Appropriate response/ difficulty or ambiguity/ some relevant information	Appropriate and unambiguous/minor errors or minor omissions	Appropriate and full response/minor errors cause no ambiguity/ TWO minor errors max.	Appropriate and correct response/task fully accomplished/NO SIGNIFICANT ERROR/ ONE minor error max.
a)	*Problema* *Maleta* (on its own)	*Tengo un problema con mi maleta.* *¿Dónde está mi maleta?*	Appropriate response **without** verbs (e.g. *maleta no aquí*)	Verb(s) essential	*Mi maleta no ha llegado/no llegó. Mi maleta no está aquí./No puedo encontrar mi maleta.* Verb essential
b)	*Londres* (on its own)	One detail only	Appropriate response **without** verbs (e.g. *vuelo de Londres siete y media*)	Verb(s) essential	**Two** clear details of flight + verb(s), e.g. *Es el vuelo IB123 de Londres. Llegué/Llegó a las siete y media.*
c)		**Two** details only, e.g. *Es grande (y) marrón.*	**Three** details & verb(s) **Four** details but no verb(s)	Appropriate response with all details & verb(s)	**Two** clear details about the suitcase, **two** clear details about the contents + verb(s), e.g. *Es grande y marrón. (Dentro) hay ropa y libros.*
d)		**One** detail only e.g. *en el centro*	**Two** details **without** verb(s), e.g. *Hotel en el centro*	**Two** details **with** verb(s), e.g. *Voy hotel en centro.*	**Two** details about the plans for the rest of the day **with** verb(s), e.g. *Voy (a ir) al hotel en el centro.*

12

CANDIDATE'S ROLE

> It is the **last** day of your holiday in Spain. You have booked an excursion for today, but the coach did not arrive. You go to the travel company to find out what has happened.
>
> **a)**   • *Tu problema.*
> **b)**   • ***Dos** detalles de la excursión.*
> **c)**   • *Tu reacción a la sugerencia de reservar otra excursión y tu razón.*
> **d)**   • !
>
> When you see ! you will have to respond to something which you have not prepared. Your teacher will play the part of the receptionist and will speak first.

■ TO HELP YOU

a) Use the rubric to help you work out the first task. Tell the receptionist you booked (reserved) an excursion and say the coach didn't arrive. You could use either the perfect or the preterite tense: first person singular 'I booked ...' and third person singular 'The coach didn't arrive'. How will you deal with 'didn't'?

b) You could mention places the excursion goes to ('It's the excursion to ...') or the times ('It leaves at ... and returns at ...') perhaps. Remember to include verbs.

c) How might you react to the offer of a place on a different excursion **tomorrow** or **next week**? Look back at the rubric. What might you have to tell the receptionist? It looks like you can't go, so say that and give your reason.

d) This is the unpredictable task! How might the role play be rounded off after complaining that you couldn't go on the excursion you've booked? What could you prepare to say in advance?

■ JOT DOWN YOUR ANSWERS

a) _____

b) _____

c) _____

d) _____

TEACHER'S ROLE

1 Begin the conversation by setting the scene and asking the candidate how you can help.
Estamos en una agencia de viajes. Yo soy el recepcionista/la recepcionista. ¿En qué puedo ayudarle?

2 Allow the candidate to say he/she has booked an excursion and that the coach did not arrive at the hotel.
Ask the candidate for details of the excursion. Elicit **two** details.
Deme algunos detalles de la excursión.

3 Allow the candidate to give **two** details of the excursion.
Apologise and say that there are no more excursions today, but there is another next week.

Ask the candidate if that would be OK and elicit a reason.
Lo siento, no hay más excursiones hoy. Hay otra la semana que viene. ¿Estará bien? . . . ¿Por qué no?

4 ❗ Allow the candidate to reject the excursion and to give a reason.
Say that it is a pity. Ask what the candidate wants to do.
¡Qué lástima! ¿Qué quiere hacer?

5 Allow the candidate to say what he/she wants to do.
End the conversation by agreeing to the candidate's suggestion.
De acuerdo.

■ MARK SCHEME

	0	1	2	3	4
	Message not communicated	Appropriate response/ difficulty or ambiguity/ some relevant information	Appropriate and unambiguous/minor errors or minor omissions	Appropriate and full response/minor errors cause no ambiguity/ TWO minor errors max.	Appropriate and correct response/task fully accomplished/NO SIGNIFICANT ERROR/ ONE minor error max.
a)	*Problema* on its own	Inappropriate tenses of verb(s) Reference only to **one** detail, e.g. *El autobús no llega.*	Reference to both elements **without** verb(s) Use of familiar form, e.g. *tu autobús no ha llegado.* No further penalty if occurs later	Reference to both elements **with** verb(s)	Clear reference to excursion booked and coach not arriving, e.g. *He reservado/Reservé una excursión (pero) el autocar no ha llegado/no llegó.*
b)		**One** detail only	**Two** details **without** verb(s), e.g. *A la capital y museos.*	**Two** details **with** verb(s)	**Two** details of the excursion, e.g. *Es la excursión a la costa (que) sale a las nueve.*
c)	*Sí*	Response only, e.g. *No*	Response + reason **without** verb(s) Reason only, e.g. *Voy a casa mañana.*	Response + reason **with** verb(s)	Response (*No* is OK on its own) + reason, e.g. *No puedo (porque) (hoy) es el último día de mis vacaciones.*
d)		*Dinero* (on its own)	Appropriate response **without** verb(s), e.g. *mi dinero por favor*	Appropriate response **with** verb(s)	Appropriate response **with** verb(s), e.g. *Quiero un reembolso/mi dinero.*

14

ROLE PLAY 8

CANDIDATE'S ROLE

> While on holiday in Spain you are on a coach trip for the day. In the afternoon you decide to return to your hotel by taxi straightaway. You speak to your Spanish guide to explain.
>
> **a)** • *Tu decisión.*
> **b)** • *Tu razón.*
> **c)** • **!**
> **d)** • *Tu opinión sobre la excursión y tu razón.*
>
> When you see **!** you will have to respond to something which you have not prepared. Your teacher will play the part of your guide and will speak first.

■ TO HELP YOU

a) The rubric could not be clearer about what you have to say for the first task. You can say 'I have decided to …' but it might be simpler to say 'I want to …', which means you'll need the first person singular of the radical changing verb *querer* followed by the other verb in the infinitive. You need to convey the idea of going by taxi 'straightaway' or 'immediately', too.

b) Use your imagination to think up a reason why you might want to interrupt this trip suddenly. Perhaps you feel unwell/sick/tired/hungry, or maybe you want to meet someone, or phone someone, or maybe you've had an accident and twisted your ankle. Keep it simple and correct, and remember to include a verb!

c) This is the unpredictable task! What might the guide ask you now that you're not taking part in the excursion for the rest of the day? Keep in mind what you've just said for the previous task, too! Make sure you use a verb and include some (simple) details.

d) Feel free to give any opinion you like about the excursion, but remember you also have to supply a reason, and that will probably require a verb (but the tense isn't important here). Which of the following might be useful opinions: interesting/fantastic/boring?

■ JOT DOWN YOUR ANSWERS

a) _____

b) _____

c) _____

d) _____

15

TEACHER'S ROLE

1 Introduce the situation, then ask the candidate how you can help.
   Estamos de excursión en España. Yo soy el/la guía. ¿En qué puedo ayudarle?

2 Allow the candidate to say that he/she wants to return to the hotel by taxi straightaway.
   Ask the candidate why.
   ¿Por qué?

3 ▌ Allow the candidate to say why he/she wants to return to the hotel by taxi straightaway. Say you understand and ask what plans the candidate has for the rest of the day. Elicit **two** details.

Ah, entiendo. ¿Qué planes tiene usted para el resto del día?

4 Allow the candidate to give **two** details about his/her plans for the rest of the day.
   Ask the candidate what he/she thinks about the trip and why.
   Está bien. ¿Qué tal la excursión? . . . ¿Por qué?

5 Allow the candidate to say what he/she thinks about the trip and why.
   End the conversation by wishing the candidate a good journey.
   Muy bien. ¡Buen viaje!

■ MARK SCHEME

	0	1	2	3	4
	Message not communicated	Appropriate response/ difficulty or ambiguity/ some relevant information	Appropriate and unambiguous/minor errors or minor omissions	Appropriate and full response/minor errors cause no ambiguity/ TWO minor errors max.	Appropriate and correct response/task fully accomplished/NO SIGNIFICANT ERROR/ ONE minor error max.
a)		**Two** elements **without** verb(s), e.g. *Al hotel en seguida.* Errors causing ambiguity (e.g. verbs are infinitives)	All elements **without** verb(s), e.g. *Taxi al hotel en seguida.* **Two** elements **with** verb(s), e.g. *Quiero volver al hotel en seguida.*	All elements **with** verb(s)	Clear explanation that the candidate wants to return to the hotel by taxi straightaway, e.g. *Quiero volver al hotel en taxi en seguida.*
b)		Errors causing ambiguity	Appropriate response **without** verb(s), e.g. *Demasiado cansado/a.*	Appropriate response Verb(s) essential	Appropriate response Verb(s) essential, e.g. *Me siento mal/Me he torcido el tobillo.*
c)		**One** detail or errors causing ambiguity, e.g. *restaurante.*	**Two** details without verb(s), e.g. *Discoteca en hotel.*	**Two** details **with** verb(s)	**Two** details **with** verb(s), e.g. *Voy a descansar en mi habitación. Leer y dormir.*
d)		Opinion (on its own) Reason (on its own)	Opinion & reason **without** verb(s), e.g. *Interesante (porque) muy bonito.*	Opinion & reason **with** verb(s), e.g. *Es interesante (porque) el costa es mucho bonita.*	Opinion & reason (which may be the same as in **b)** above). Verb(s) essential, e.g. *Es/Fue (muy) interesante (porque) la costa es muy bonita.*

CANDIDATE'S ROLE

You and your Spanish friend decide to go on holiday together. Your Spanish friend wants to go skiing, but you are not sure.

a)   • ***Dos*** *detalles de tus vacaciones del año pasado.*
b)   • *Tu opinión sobre esas vacaciones y tu razón.*
c)   • ***Dos*** *opiniones del esquí.*
d)   • ❗

When you see ❗ you will have to respond to something which you have not prepared. Your teacher will play the part of your friend and will speak first.

■ TO HELP YOU

a) The task here is to mention **two** things about your holiday last year. Use the preterite tense to talk about where you went, what you did/saw/visited, etc. Keep your opinions till the next task.

b) There are lots of ways to express an opinion (positive or negative), but remember you have to give a reason, too. You could add a simple adjective to the phrases *Lo pasé* ... ('I had a ... time') or *Mis vacaciones fueron* ... ('My holidays were ...'). In the second of these examples the adjective will be feminine plural! For the reason, choose a favourite activity (in the past tense), describe a place you went to (in the present tense), or say what you liked (*gustar* in the preterite tense).

c) Now you have to give **two** opinions about skiing. The rubric suggests that you're not sure about skiing, so that might be something to think about. Perhaps you could give mixed opinions and link them with *pero*. How about: fun/expensive/exciting/dangerous/easy, for example?

d) This is the unpredictable task! Given that your friend thinks you're not sure about skiing, and you're both discussing a holiday together, what might he/she ask you next?

■ JOT DOWN YOUR ANSWERS

a) _____

b) _____

c) _____

d) _____

TEACHER'S ROLE

1 Begin the conversation by explaining the situation and then ask the candidate how he/she spent his/her holidays last year. Elicit **two** details.
Estás hablando de las vacaciones con tu amigo español/tu amiga española. Yo soy tu amigo/amiga. ¿Qué hiciste durante las vacaciones del año pasado?

2 Allow the candidate to give **two** details about how he/she spent his/her holidays last year. Ask if he/she enjoyed the holiday. Elicit a reason.
¿Qué tal lo pasaste? . . . ¿Por qué?

3 Allow the candidate to say if he/she enjoyed the holiday and to give a reason.
Say you like going skiing and ask the candidate what he/she thinks. Elicit **two** opinions.
A mí me gusta mucho el esquí. ¿Qué te parece?

4 ⚠ Allow the candidate to give **two** opinions about skiing.
Accept the candidate's opinions. Ask what he/she suggests instead and why.
Vale. ¿Qué vamos a hacer entonces? . . . ¿Por qué?

5 Allow the candidate to say what he/she suggests instead and to give a reason.
End the conversation by accepting the candidate's preference.
Vale, como quieras.

■ MARK SCHEME

	0	1	2	3	4
	Message not communicated	Appropriate response/ difficulty or ambiguity/ some relevant information	Appropriate and unambiguous/minor errors or minor omissions	Appropriate and full response/minor errors cause no ambiguity/ TWO minor errors max.	Appropriate and correct response/task fully accomplished/NO SIGNIFICANT ERROR/ ONE minor error max.
a)		**One** detail only	**Two** details **without** verb(s), e.g. *España con mi familia.*	**Two** details **with** verb(s)	**Two** details about last year's holiday **with** verb(s), e.g. *Fui a España con mi familia/nadé en el mar/tomé el sol en la playa,* etc.
b)		Opinion only Reason only	Opinion and reason **without** verb(s), e.g. *¡Estupendo! – discotecas excelentes.*	Opinion and reason **with** verb(s)	Opinion and reason **with** verb(s), e.g. *(Lo pasé) muy bien (porque) me gustó el parque de atracciones.*
c)		**One** opinion only	**Two** opinions **without** verb(s), e.g. *Fácil (pero) caro.*	**Two** opinions **with** verb(s)	**Two** opinions about skiing **with** verb(s), e.g. *Es divertido (pero) peligroso.*
d)		Activity on its own	**One** activity plus a reason **without** verb(s), e.g. *La Costa del sol – discotecas.*	**One** activity plus a reason **with** verb(s)	**One** alternative activity plus a reason **with** verb(s) Infinitive OK e.g. *Vamos a la playa (porque) hay mucho que hacer.*

CANDIDATE'S ROLE

You are talking with your Spanish friend about Christmas and New Year holidays.

a) • *El día de Navidad del año pasado – dónde y con quién.*

b) • ***Dos*** *regalos y **dos** actividades.*

c) • ***Dos*** *tipos de comida y **una** bebida para Navidad en tu casa.*

d) • **!**

When you see **!** you will have to respond to something which you have not prepared. Your teacher will play the part of your friend and will speak first.

■ TO HELP YOU

a) The guidance is very clear here. Say where you spent Christmas Day last year and who you were with. There are two verbs for 'spend': *gastar* (for money) and *pasar* (for time). Make sure you use the right one! Use the preterite tense, choose any activity you like, and perhaps use a Spanish word (e.g. family members/friends) rather than mention people by name.

b) Again the guidance is very clear here. Mention **two** presents you got (received) and **two** things you did. Use the preterite tense and keep the phrases fairly simple.

c) You can use the present tense for this task. Make sure you mention **two** things you eat and **one** thing you drink. You could use either the first person singular or plural of the verbs here.

d) This is the unpredictable task! Perhaps the rubric will give you a small clue, if you notice that so far in the role play you've only spoken about Christmas.

■ JOT DOWN YOUR ANSWERS

a) _____

b) _____

c) _____

d) _____

TEACHER'S ROLE

1 Begin the conversation by explaining the situation and then ask the candidate to tell you where and with whom he/she spent Christmas day last year.
Estás hablando de la Navidad con tu amigo español/tu amiga española. Yo soy tu amigo/amiga. Háblame del día de Navidad del año pasado.

2 Allow the candidate to say where he/she spent Christmas last year and with whom. Ask what presents the candidate received and what he/she did during the day. Elicit information about **two** presents and **two** activities. *¿Qué regalos recibiste? . . . Y ¿qué hiciste durante el día?*

3 Allow the candidate to mention **two** presents received and also **two** things he/she did. Ask what he/she or members of his/her family eat and drink on Christmas Day. Elicit **two** items of food and **one** drink.
Háblame de la comida en tu casa el día de Navidad. . . . Y ¿para beber?

4 ⚠ Allow the candidate to mention **two** things normally eaten and **one** thing drunk by him/her or members of the family on Christmas Day. Ask what he/she normally does on New Year's Eve. Elicit **two** activities.
¿Y qué haces normalmente en Nochevieja, es decir el 31 de diciembre?

5 Allow the candidate to mention **two** activities he/she normally does on New Year's Eve. End the conversation by saying that is interesting. *¡Qué interesante!*

■ MARK SCHEME

	0	1	2	3	4
	Message not communicated	Appropriate response/ difficulty or ambiguity/ some relevant information	Appropriate and unambiguous/minor errors or minor omissions	Appropriate and full response/minor errors cause no ambiguity/ TWO minor errors max.	Appropriate and correct response/task fully accomplished/NO SIGNIFICANT ERROR/ ONE minor error max.
a)	*Navidad* (on its own)	**One** detail only Wrong verb tense	**Two** clear details **without** verb(s), e.g. *En casa con familia.*	**Two** clear details **with** past tense verb(s)	**Two** clear details about where Christmas was spent and with whom – past tense verb(s) must be included, e.g. *Pasé (el día de) Navidad en casa con mi familia.*
b)		Omission of more than one element	**Two** presents and **two** appropriate activities **without** verb(s) Omission of one element only	**Two** presents and **two** appropriate activities **with** verb(s)	**Two** presents and **two** appropriate activities **with** verb(s), e.g. *Recibí dinero y videos; vi la tele y escuché música.*
c)		One or two items only	All three items clear **without** verb(s)	All three items clear **with** verb(s)	All three items clear with verb(s). Past or present tenses, but must be consistent, e.g. *Comemos pavo y patatas; bebemos cerveza.*
d)		**One** activity only	Appropriate response **without** verb(s), e.g. *discoteca y copas*	**Two** appropriate activities **with** verb(s)	**Two** appropriate activities **with** verb(s); verb may include activity, e.g. *Voy a una fiesta y bailo.*

CANDIDATE'S ROLE

Your Spanish friend is due to come to stay with you next week. Unfortunately, you now have to telephone your friend to cancel the visit as there is a problem at home. You also need to make arrangements for your friend to visit at another time.

a) • *Razón por la llamada.*
b) • *Detalle del problema.*
c) • *Planes para otra visita.*
d) •

When you see ▊ you will have to respond to something which you have not prepared. Your teacher will play the part of your friend and will speak first.

■ TO HELP YOU

a) In this task you simply have to tell your Spanish friend: 'you cannot come to visit me'. Leave the rest of the information in the rubric to the next tasks. The key verb here will be *poder*, and you'll need the second person singular. Remember it's radical changing, and leave the second verb in the infinitive. Where will you put the negative *no* and the object pronoun *me*?

b) The only guidance you're given is that there's a problem at home, so think of something fairly simple to say. Perhaps someone is unwell, or you have important exams or work experience, for example. You'll need to include a verb.

c) This is your opportunity to rearrange the visit. Offer your friend a different date and ask if he/she can visit you then, or tell him/her when you are free and ask if that's possible.

d) This is the unpredictable task! Apart from practical arrangements what else might your Spanish friend want to know ahead of the visit? Put yourself in the position of receiving a guest and see if that helps.

■ JOT DOWN YOUR ANSWERS

a) _____

b) _____

c) _____

d) _____

TEACHER'S ROLE

1 Begin the conversation by explaining the situation and then answer the telephone and ask the candidate what the problem is.
Estás llamando por teléfono a tu amigo español/tu amiga española. Yo soy tu amigo/amiga.
¡Hola! ¿Tienes algún problema?

2 Allow the candidate to say that you cannot come to visit next week.
Ask why not.
¿Por qué no?

3 Allow the candidate to explain why you cannot come to visit next week.
Say you are disappointed and ask what arrangements could be made for you to visit at another time.

¡Qué pena! ¿Qué planes podemos hacer para mi visita, entonces?

4 🗨 Allow the candidate to suggest what arrangements could be made for you to visit at another time.
Accept the candidate's suggestion and ask him/her what you could do during your visit. Elicit **two** activities.
Vale. ¿Qué actividades podemos hacer durante mis vacaciones allí?

5 Allow the candidate to suggest **two** activities.
End the conversation by responding positively to the candidate's suggestions.
¡Qué bien!

■ MARK SCHEME

	0	1	2	3	4
	Message not communicated	Appropriate response/ difficulty or ambiguity/ some relevant information	Appropriate and unambiguous/minor errors or minor omissions	Appropriate and full response/minor errors cause no ambiguity/ TWO minor errors max.	Appropriate and correct response/task fully accomplished/NO SIGNIFICANT ERROR/ ONE minor error max.
a)		Ambiguous response (e.g. *no visita*)	Explanation **without** verb(s), e.g. *Tu visita no posible.*	Explanation **with** verb(s)	Explanation **with** verbs, e.g. *No puedes visitarme (la semana que viene).*
b)		Ambiguous response, e.g. *enferma*	Explanation of problem at home **without** verb(s), e.g. *Madre enferma.* Incorrect verb e.g. *Mi madre (etc.) es enferma.*	Explanation of problem at home **with** verb(s)	Explanation of problem at home **with** verb(s), e.g. *Mi madre está enferma./Tengo exámenes (muy) importantes.*
c)			New arrangements **without** verb(s), e.g. new date only	New arrangements **with** verb(s)	New arrangements **with** verb(s), e.g. *¿Puedes venir en julio?/¿El 15 de agosto es posible?*
d)		**One** activity only	**Two** activities **without** verb(s), e.g. *Piscina y club de jóvenes.*	**Two** activities **with** verb(s)	**Two** activities – full verbal response for at least ONE of the activities, e.g. *Podremos ir a la bolera . . . y al cine también.*

CANDIDATE'S ROLE

> You are in a restaurant in Spain. You and your Spanish friend have just sat down. The people at the next table start smoking. You are really keen to eat at this restaurant today, but you do not want to sit near smokers.
>
> **a)** • *Tu problema.*
> **b)** • ***Dos*** *opiniones sobre el tabaco.*
> **c)** • *Tu reacción a la sugerencia de ir a otro restaurante y tu razón.*
> **d)** • 🔲
>
> When you see 🔲 you will have to respond to something which you have not prepared. Your teacher will play the part of your friend and will speak first.

■ TO HELP YOU

a) The guidance in the rubric indicates that you need to tell your Spanish friend that the people at the next table are smoking. There are two words for 'people' in Spanish: *personas* (if you need to count them) and *gente* (when referring to them in general terms). Which one would you use here? Remember that *personas* is feminine plural, and *gente* is feminine singular. So which part of the verb will you need?

b) Now you can give your opinions about smoking, and from this situation it sounds as though you're not really in favour, so you'll have to give negative opinions. What could you say to your friend? That smoking is bad for your health, you don't like the smoke, it's dirty or expensive, perhaps? Use the infinitive of the verb to refer to 'smoking', if you want.

c) This task could also be influenced by the rubric, so if your friend suggests going to another restaurant, how might you react? 'I am really keen (would really like) . . .' sounds like an opportunity to use the conditional tense of the impersonal verb *gustar* strengthened by the adverb *mucho*. Remember you need a reaction **and** a reason.

d) This is the unpredictable task! The situation hasn't been resolved satisfactorily yet, so maybe you can think of a solution that means you can still eat in this restaurant. A useful verb might be *poder* – present tense ('we can . . .') or perhaps conditional ('we could . . .').

■ JOT DOWN YOUR ANSWERS

a) _____

b) _____

c) _____

d) _____

TEACHER'S ROLE

1 Begin the conversation by explaining the situation and asking the candidate what the problem is.
Estamos en un restaurante en España. Yo soy tu amigo español/tu amiga española.
¿Qué te pasa?

2 Allow the candidate to say that the people at the next table are smoking.
Say it does not bother you and ask why it bothers the candidate. Elicit **two** reasons.
A mí no me importa. ¿Por qué no te gusta?

3 Allow the candidate to give **two** reasons for being bothered by smoking.
Say OK and suggest you go to another restaurant.

Ask what the candidate thinks about your suggestion. Elicit a reason.
Vale. Podemos ir a otro restaurante. ¿Qué te parece? . . . ¿Por qué (no)?

4 ⚠ Allow the candidate to reject (or accept) the suggestion to go to another restaurant and to give a reason.
Agree with the candidate and ask what the candidate suggests to solve the problem.
Muy bien. ¿Qué hacemos?

5 Allow the candidate to suggest a solution.
End the conversation by agreeing to the candidate's solution.
Buena idea.

■ MARK SCHEME

	0	1	2	3	4
	Message not communicated	Appropriate response/ difficulty or ambiguity/ some relevant information	Appropriate and unambiguous/minor errors or minor omissions	Appropriate and full response/minor errors cause no ambiguity/ TWO minor errors max.	Appropriate and correct response/task fully accomplished/NO SIGNIFICANT ERROR/ ONE minor error max.
a)	*Problema* on its own	Ambiguous response, e.g. *Fumar en la mesa.*	Full response **without** verb(s) Omission of next table + rest correct	Full response **with** verb(s)	Full response **with** verb(s), e.g. *Están fumando en la mesa de al lado.*
b)	Inappropriate response, e.g. *Me gusta fumar.*	**One** opinion only	**Two** negative opinions **without** verb(s)	**Two** negative opinions **with** verb(s)	**Two** negative opinions **with** verb(s), e.g. *Es malo (para la salud) y sucio.*
c)		Rejection only Ambiguity or difficulty present *Sí* (on its own)	Reason only Appropriate response **without** verb(s)	As in 4 marks column **with** verb(s)	Clear rejection (*No* on own OK) + reason with verb(s) OR clear acceptance (e.g. *Sí, buena idea*) + reason which should not just repeat previous statements (e.g. *No me gusta el humo*)
d)		If they wish to leave: *Sí + vamos a otro restaurante.*	Appropriate response **without** verb(s), e.g. *otra mesa.*	As in 4 marks column **with** verb(s)	Appropriate response + verb(s). If they wish to leave, look for new reasons (not *otro restaurante* but e.g. *italiano/de enfrente*)

24

© John Murray

CANDIDATE'S ROLE

You have a summer job in Spain. Unfortunately you have had a slight accident so you telephone your employer to explain why you cannot go to work today.

a) • *Razón por tu llamada.*

b) • *Descripción del accidente – dónde y cuándo.*

c) • *Dos detalles de tus heridas.*

d) • **!**

When you see **!** you will have to respond to something which you have not prepared. Your teacher will play the part of your employer and will speak first.

■ TO HELP YOU

a) You need to say something like: 'I can't go to work. I've had an accident.' Use the first person singular of the (radical changing) verb *poder* followed by the second verb in the infinitive. You'll need the perfect tense perhaps, to say 'I have had …'. Since 'to have an accident' uses *tener*, what other verb for 'have' will you need for the auxiliary verb in the perfect tense?

b) Now you should describe the accident briefly, including where and when it happened. Keep it fairly simple, perhaps something like: 'I fell on the stairs (in the street/sports centre) this morning (yesterday)', which will allow you to mention your actual injuries in the next task.

c) You need to give **two** details, so perhaps you could mention two different injuries or two parts of your body. You could use a mixture of tenses, too. For example, 'I broke/twisted/hurt/cut …' and/or 'I have a sore leg/arm/knee (etc)'. Remember the special phrases you need for this. It's also usual to refer to parts of the body with the definite article (*el/la/los/las*).

d) This is the unpredictable task! Now that you've told your employer that you can't come to work today, what might he/she want to know next?

■ JOT DOWN YOUR ANSWERS

a) _____

b) _____

c) _____

d) _____

ROLE PLAY 13

TEACHER'S ROLE

1 Begin the conversation by explaining the situation and answering the telephone.
Estás en España. Estás llamando por teléfono a tu jefe/jefa. Yo soy el jefe/la jefa. ¡Dígame!

2 Allow the candidate to say he/she has had an accident and cannot go to work.
Ask the candidate what happened, where and when.
¿Qué pasó exactamente? . . . ¿Dónde? . . . ¿Cuándo?

3 Allow the candidate to say where and when the accident happened.
Ask the candidate for details about the injuries he/she has. Elicit **two** details.
¿Está herido/herida? ¿Qué le pasa exactamente?

4 ❗ Allow the candidate to give **two** details about his/her injuries.
Sympathise and ask what plans the candidate has for returning to work.
¡Qué lástima! ¿Qué planes tiene para volver al trabajo?

5 Allow the candidate to say what his/her plans for returning to work are.
End the conversation by saying that you hope the candidate will be better soon.
Que se mejore pronto.

■ MARK SCHEME

	0	1	2	3	4
	Message not communicated	Appropriate response/ difficulty or ambiguity/ some relevant information	Appropriate and unambiguous/minor errors or minor omissions	Appropriate and full response/minor errors cause no ambiguity/ TWO minor errors max.	Appropriate and correct response/task fully accomplished/NO SIGNIFICANT ERROR/ ONE minor error max.
a)	*Accidente* on its own *Trabajo* on its own	Only one element	Both elements **without** verb(s), e.g. *Mi trabajo imposible porque accidente.*	Both elements **with** verb(s), e.g. *No puedo ir el trabajo. He tenido accidente.*	Reference to not being able to work and to accident, with verb(s), e.g. *No puedo ir al trabajo. He tenido un accidente.*
b)		Two/three elements + ambiguity Two elements only No reference to where and when, but one detail of accident clearly conveyed	All three elements with errors Two elements without errors	All three elements **with** verb(s)	One element of description + when + where, conveyed **with** verb(s), e.g. *(Me) caí por la escalera esta mañana.*
c)		**One** detail only	**Two** details about injuries **without** verb(s), e.g. *Dolor de pie y brazo.*	**Two** details about injuries, **with** verb(s)	**Two** details about injuries, **with** verb(s); variety of tenses possible, e.g. *Me torcí el tobillo (y) me duele la pierna.*
d)		Appropriate response with ambiguity	Details of plans **without** verb(s)	Plans to go back to work **with** verb(s)	Plans to go back to work **with** verb(s), e.g. *Espero volver al trabajo el lunes que viene.*

CANDIDATE'S ROLE

> You are in Barcelona airport on your way home. You have just realised that you have left your bag in the hotel. You telephone the hotel and speak to the receptionist.
>
> **a)** • *Tu problema.*
> **b)** • *Tus **dos** actividades en el hotel esta mañana.*
> **c)** • !
> **d)** • *Tu solución para obtener la bolsa.*
>
> When you see ! you will have to respond to something which you have not prepared. Your teacher will play the part of the receptionist and will speak first.

■ TO HELP YOU

a) Tell the receptionist: 'I have left (forgotten) my bag in the hotel'. You'll need the perfect tense for either of these verbs. Which is the correct auxiliary verb for 'have' in the perfect tense: *tener*, *haber* or *tomar*?

b) What did you do in the hotel this morning? Perhaps you had your bag with you, and could say: 'I went to the .../I ate in the .../I read in the .../I watched .../or I played ...'. You'll need to use the preterite tense, so choose the first person singular of verbs you know confidently.

c) This is the unpredictable task! What will it be important for the receptionist to know if he/she is going to be able to find your bag? How much detail can you supply? (Remember there are four marks available for the task!)

d) Now you need to make arrangements to get the bag back. Perhaps you could tell him/her you will return to the hotel by taxi (future tense) or maybe you could ask him/her to send it to you (*poder* as a question, third person singular).

■ JOT DOWN YOUR ANSWERS

a) _____

b) _____

c) _____

d) _____

TEACHER'S ROLE

1 Introduce the situation, then answer the telephone.
Estamos en España. Yo soy un/una recepcionista.
¡Diga! Hotel España.

2 Allow the candidate to explain the problem.
Ask the candidate to say what he/she did in the hotel this morning. Elicit **two** details.
¿Qué hizo usted en el hotel esta mañana?

3 🔳 Allow the candidate to give **two** details about what he/she did in the hotel this morning.
Ask the candidate to describe the bag and its contents. Elicit **two** details about the bag and **two** details about the contents.
Describa la bolsa por favor. . . . Y ¿dentro de la bolsa?

4 Allow the candidate to give **two** details about the bag and **two** details about the contents.
Say that you have the bag. Ask the candidate what he/she wants to do to get the bag back.
Ah, sí. Tengo la bolsa aquí. ¿Qué hago con la bolsa?

5 Allow the candidate to say what he/she wants to do to get the bag back.
End the conversation by agreeing to the candidate's suggestion.
Muy bien.

■ MARK SCHEME

	0	1	2	3	4
	Message not communicated	Appropriate response/ difficulty or ambiguity/ some relevant information	Appropriate and unambiguous/minor errors or minor omissions	Appropriate and full response/minor errors cause no ambiguity/ TWO minor errors max.	Appropriate and correct response/task fully accomplished/NO SIGNIFICANT ERROR/ ONE minor error max.
a)		Errors causing ambiguity, e.g. *Tengo perdido mi bolsa en el/un hotel.*	Full response **without** verb(s)	Full response **with** verb(s), e.g. *He dejado el bolsa en hotel.*	Full response with verb in perfect or preterite, e.g. *He dejado/Dejé mi bolsa en el hotel.*
b)		**One** detail only	**Two** details about activities in the hotel (grounds) **without** verb(s) e.g. *Restaurante (y) piscina.*	**Two** details about activities in the hotel (grounds) **with** verb(s) e.g. *Vi televisión (y) jugué el tenis.*	Clear reference to **two** details about activities in the hotel (grounds); verb is essential, e.g. *Comí en el restaurante (y) jugué al tenis.* (Accept nouns, e.g. *natación*)
c)		Only **two** details	Only **three** details	Clear reference to **four** details	Clear description of the bag and its contents; **four** details are essential, e.g. *Es pequeña y roja. (Dentro) hay discos compactos y tebeos.*
d)		Errors causing ambiguity	Appropriate response **without** verb(s)	Appropriate response **with** verb(s)	Appropriate response **with** verb(s), e.g. *¿Puede usted mandar mi bolsa a Inglaterra?*

ROLE PLAY 15

CANDIDATE'S ROLE

> You would like a summer job in Spain for the months of July and August. You telephone your Spanish friend for help.
>
> **a)** • *Razón por tu llamada.*
> **b)** • ***Dos*** *detalles de tu experiencia laboral.*
> **c)** • !
> **d)** • *Planes para tu tiempo libre (**dos** actividades).*
>
> When you see ! you will have to respond to something which you have not prepared. Your teacher will play the part of your friend and will speak first.

■ TO HELP YOU

a) The rubric gives you very clear guidance here. Give all the details including place and months, with a verb!

b) You need to give **two** details of your work experience. The present tense or the past tense are acceptable. You could mention the job, the place of work, your duties, your hours of work, etc. Keep the information as simple and correct as possible.

c) This is the unpredictable task! Remember you are asking your Spanish friend for help, and all that's mentioned in the rubric is a reference to 'Spain' as a whole.

d) Life is not all work, so now you can mention what plans you have for your free time while you are in Spain! Say something like 'I am going to ...' (present tense of *ir* plus infinitives) or 'I would like to ...' (*querer* – present tense; *gustar* – conditional tense; plus infinitives). Remember to mention **two** activities!

■ JOT DOWN YOUR ANSWERS

a) _____

b) _____

c) _____

d) _____

TEACHER'S ROLE

1 Begin the conversation by explaining the situation and asking the candidate how you can help.
Estás llamando por teléfono a tu amigo español/tu amiga española. Yo soy tu amigo/amiga.
¡Hola! ¿En qué puedo ayudarte?

2 Allow the candidate to say he/she wants a job in Spain in July and August. Ask what work experience he/she has had. Elicit **two** details.
¿Qué tipo de experiencia laboral has tenido exactamente?

3 ⚠ Allow the candidate to give **two** details about the work experience he/she has had.
Ask in which part of Spain the candidate wants to work. Elicit a reason.

¿En qué región de España quieres trabajar? . . . ¿Por qué?

4 Allow the candidate to say in which part of Spain he/she wants to work and why.
Ask the candidate what he/she is going to do in his/her spare time whilst in Spain.
¿Qué planes tienes para tu tiempo libre aquí en España?

5 Allow the candidate to give **two** activities he/she is going to do in his/her spare time in Spain.
End the conversation by saying you will call him/her when you have more information.
Te llamaré cuando tenga más información.

■ MARK SCHEME

	0	1	2	3	4
	Message not communicated	Appropriate response/ difficulty or ambiguity/ some relevant information	Appropriate and unambiguous/minor errors or minor omissions	Appropriate and full response/minor errors cause no ambiguity/ TWO minor errors max.	Appropriate and correct response/task fully accomplished/NO SIGNIFICANT ERROR/ ONE minor error max.
a)		Omission of more than one detail (e.g. in Spain, and the months)	Omission of **one** detail (e.g. in Spain, or the months)	Full response **with** verb(s)	Full and correct response **with** verb(s), e.g. *Quiero un trabajo en España durante julio y agosto.*
b)		Only **one** detail	**Two** details of his/her work experience **without** verb(s)	**Two** details of his/her work experience **with** verb(s)	**Two** details of his/her work experience with verb(s); present tense OK, e.g. *Soy dependiente/a en una tienda.*
c)		Omission of reason	Part of Spain and reason **without** verb(s), e.g. *Costa del Sol – playas bonitas.*	Part of Spain he/she wants to work in and reason	Part of Spain he/she wants to work in with reason, e.g. *Norte/ sur, (porque) es muy bonito/hace mucho sol* (etc.)
d)		Only **one** activity given Two nouns *Me gusta* plus one activity	*Me gusta* + **two** activities	**Two** spare time activities **with** verb(s)	**Two** spare time activities; infinitive(s) OK, e.g. *(Voy a) ir a la discoteca y jugar al tenis.*

CANDIDATE'S ROLE

> You are talking to your Spanish friend about your past work experience.
>
> **a)** • *Tus prácticas laborales – dónde y las horas de trabajo.*
> **b)** • *Tu opinión sobre tu jefe y razón.*
> **c)** • *Tu trabajo – **dos** actividades.*
> **d)** • ❗
>
> When you see ❗ you will have to respond to something which you have not prepared. Your teacher will play the part of your friend and will speak first.

■ TO HELP YOU

a) The important thing to notice in the rubric is that you are talking about **past** work experience, so you'll need to use a past tense, probably the preterite. If you haven't actually done any work experience, use your imagination. Use the first person singular of any verbs you use: 'to work', and maybe 'to start' and 'to finish' if you want. You could also say 'from (one time) until (another time)'. Note that in this case you will need the imperfect.

b) You can give any opinion you like, and it can be quite simple, but remember that you have to give a reason for it. So if you think the boss is kind/strict/lazy/quiet, for example, back it up with a statement that justifies it. You can keep to the present tense for both parts here.

c) Again remember that you're talking about **past** work experience, so you'll probably need **two** verbs in the preterite tense. A lot depends on what work you did, but choose two fairly straightforward activities. Think of some that might be common to most jobs, perhaps.

d) This is the unpredictable task! There's not much additional information in the rubric to help you, so maybe the topic stays on work experience.

■ JOT DOWN YOUR ANSWERS

a) _____

b) _____

c) _____

d) _____

TEACHER'S ROLE

1 Introduce the situation, then ask the candidate what he/she did for work experience.
Estás hablando con tu amigo español/tu amiga española. Yo soy tu amigo/amiga.
¿Qué hiciste para tus prácticas laborales?

2 Allow the candidate to say where he/she did work experience and to say what the working hours were.
Ask the candidate what his/her boss is like and why he/she says that.
¿Qué tal tu jefe? . . . ¿Por qué dices eso?

3 Allow the candidate to say what his/her boss is like and why.
Ask the candidate what type of work he/she did.
Elicit **two** activities.
¿Qué tipo de trabajo hiciste?

4 ❗ Allow the candidate to say **two** things he/she did during work experience.
Ask the candidate what he/she thinks about work experience and why.
¿Cuál es tu opinión sobre las prácticas laborales?
. . . ¿Por qué dices eso?

5 Allow the candidate to say what he/she thinks about work experience and why.
End the conversation by saying you liked your work experience.
A mí me gustaron mis prácticas laborales.

■ MARK SCHEME

	0	1	2	3	4
	Message not communicated	Appropriate response/ difficulty or ambiguity/ some relevant information	Appropriate and unambiguous/minor errors or minor omissions	Appropriate and full response/minor errors cause no ambiguity/ TWO minor errors max.	Appropriate and correct response/task fully accomplished/NO SIGNIFICANT ERROR/ ONE minor error max.
a)		One element only in past tense Two elements in present tense	Full details with mixed tenses	Full details with past tense of verb(s)	Place and hours of work; past tense of verb(s) essential, e.g. *Trabajé en un supermercado. Empezaba a las nueve y terminaba a las cinco.*
b)		Opinion only	Opinion and reason **without** verb(s)	Opinion and reason **with** verb(s)	Opinion and reason **with** verb(s), e.g. *Es callado (porque) no habla mucho.*
c)		Only **one** activity	**Two** activities **without** verb(s)	**Two** activities Past tense essential	**Two** activities; past tense essential, e.g. *Hablé con los clientes (y) usé el ordenador.*
d)		Opinion alone Reason alone	Opinion + reason **without** verb(s)	Opinion + reason	Opinion + reason, e.g. *Son útiles (porque) son buenos para el trabajo futuro.*

CANDIDATE'S ROLE

> You have arranged a holiday job as a receptionist in a Spanish hotel.
> The job starts on 13th June. Unfortunately you cannot start on that date.
> You really want a job in Spain so you telephone the hotel manager.
>
> **a)**   • *Tu problema.*
> **b)**   • *Tu razón.*
> **c)**   • *Tu sugerencia para resolver el problema.*
> **d)**   • ❗
>
> When you see ❗ you will have to respond to something which you
> have not prepared. Your teacher will play the part of the manager and
> will speak first.

■ TO HELP YOU

a) Using the rubric you can work out that you need to tell the manager: 'I cannot start (my) work on 13th June.' Begin with the first person singular of *poder* and follow it with an infinitive. To say 'on' with the date in Spanish just say 'the', followed by '13', followed by 'of June'.

b) You are free to offer any reason you wish. Perhaps someone is unwell, or you have important exams, or you have different travel plans, for example. You'll need to include a verb.

c) It is also up to you to suggest a solution to this problem. Perhaps you could say when you can start work/when you will be free/when you will arrive and ask if that's okay. Or just ask if you can start on a different date.

d) This is the unpredictable task! The rubric emphasises that you **really** want a job, so is there a possibility that they might not keep the job of receptionist open for you? Is that your only option?

■ JOT DOWN YOUR ANSWERS

a) _____

b) _____

c) _____

d) _____

TEACHER'S ROLE

1 Begin the conversation by introducing the situation and asking how you can help.
Estás llamando por teléfono al director/al la directora de un hotel en España. Yo soy el director/la directora. ¿En qué puedo ayudarle?

2 Allow the candidate to say he/she cannot begin work on 13th June.
Ask the candidate why he/she cannot start on that date.
¿Por qué no puede empezar en esa fecha?

3 Allow the candidate to say why he/she cannot begin work on that date.
Ask the candidate what he/she wants to do.
Bueno, ¿qué quiere hacer?

4 ▣ Allow the candidate to say what he/she wants to do to resolve the problem.
Say you will not be able to offer the job of receptionist.
Ask what other type of work the candidate could do and what experience the candidate has.
Como recepcionista no será posible. ¿Qué otro tipo de trabajo podría hacer? ¿Qué experiencia tiene?

5 Allow the candidate to say what other type of work he/she could do and what experience he/she has.
End the conversation by accepting the suggestion.
Está bien.

▣ MARK SCHEME

	0	1	2	3	4
	Message not communicated	Appropriate response/ difficulty or ambiguity/ some relevant information	Appropriate and unambiguous/minor errors or minor omissions	Appropriate and full response/minor errors cause no ambiguity/ TWO minor errors max.	Appropriate and correct response/task fully accomplished/NO SIGNIFICANT ERROR/ ONE minor error max.
a)		*Tengo problema con el trabajo.*	Full response **without** verb(s)	Full response **with** verb(s)	Clear statement that he/she cannot (begin) work on date arranged, e.g. *No puedo empezar el 13 de junio.* Verb(s) essential.
b)		Errors causing ambiguity, e.g. *Enfermo* (on its own)	Clear reason **without** verb(s) *Exámenes* (on its own)	Clear reason, **with** verb(s)	Clear reason for not being able to start work, **with** verb(s), e.g. *Tengo (unos) exámenes (muy) importantes.*
c)		Errors causing ambiguity, e.g. *¿Agosto?* (on its own)	Appropriate response **without** verb(s)	Appropriate response **with** verb(s)	Appropriate response **with** verb(s), e.g. *Voy a llegar el 20 de junio. ¿Está bien?/¿Puedo empezar una semana más tarde?*
d)		One element only, e.g. *Camarero/a* (on its own)	Type of work + experience, **without** verb(s)	Type of work + experience, **with** verb(s)	Type of work (single word OK – e.g. *camarero/a*) + experience, **with** verb(s), e.g. *(Puedo ser) camarero/a (porque) he trabajado en un restaurante.*

34

ROLE PLAY 18

CANDIDATE'S ROLE

> Your Spanish friend is carrying out a survey on popular TV programmes.
>
> **a)** • *Tu programa favorito – día y hora.*
> **b)** • ***Dos** detalles del programa.*
> **c)** • *Tu personaje preferido y descripción (**tres** detalles).*
> **d)** • !
>
> When you see **!** you will have to respond to something which you have not prepared. Your teacher will play the part of your friend and will speak first.

■ TO HELP YOU

a) First of all it would be a good idea to name your favourite TV programme, and then go on to say what day and what time it's on. 'My favourite programme is/is called …' (and just give its name in English). 'I watch it/They show it on … (day) at … (time).' Which comes first in Spanish – 'favourite' or 'programme'? Where will you put the object pronoun *lo* (for it)? And just use *el* for 'on (day)'.

b) For this task you need to give **two** pieces of information about the programme, for example: the type of programme it is (music/sport/soap opera, etc.) or perhaps what it's about (families/animals/a police station/a hospital, etc.), and so on. There's a very useful phrase for 'it's about …'.

c) Choose one of the characters in the programme, give his/her name and **three** details about him/her, for example: profession/birthday/family details/or a description of him/her (hair and eyes), etc. Remember that you're talking about somebody else, so your verbs will have to be in the third person.

d) This is the unpredictable task! After giving all these factual details, what else might you need to give? And always be prepared to give reasons!

■ JOT DOWN YOUR ANSWERS

a) _____

b) _____

c) _____

d) _____

TEACHER'S ROLE

1 Begin the conversation by explaining the situation and then ask the candidate what his/her favourite TV programme is. Elicit the day and time he/she watches it.

Estás hablando de los programas de televisión con tu amigo español/tu amiga española. Yo soy tu amigo/amiga.

¿Cuál es tu programa de televisión favorito? . . . ¿Qué día lo ponen y a qué hora?

2 Allow the candidate to name his/her favourite TV programme and the day and the time he/she watches it. Ask him/her to tell you something about the programme. Elicit **two** details.

Háblame del programa.

3 Allow the candidate to give you **two** details about the programme.

Ask the candidate to name his/her favourite character in the programme, and to describe him/her. Elicit **three** details in terms of physical description and/or personality.

¿Cómo se llama el personaje que prefieres en el programa? . . . ¿Cómo es?/Descríbelo.

4 ❗ Allow the candidate to name his/her favourite character, and to give **three** details describing him/her. Ask why he/she particularly likes this programme. Elicit **two** reasons.

¿Y por qué te gusta tanto este programa?

5 Allow the candidate to give **two** reasons why he/she likes the programme. End the conversation by saying that it sounds really interesting.

Muy bien. Parece muy interesante.

■ MARK SCHEME

	0	1	2	3	4
	Message not communicated	Appropriate response/ difficulty or ambiguity/ some relevant information	Appropriate and unambiguous/minor errors or minor omissions	Appropriate and full response/minor errors cause no ambiguity/ TWO minor errors max.	Appropriate and correct response/task fully accomplished/NO SIGNIFICANT ERROR/ ONE minor error max.
a)		**One** or **two** details only	**Three** clear details **without** verb(s) e.g. *EastEnders domingo a las dos.*	**Three** clear details required; verb(s) must be present	**Three** clear details required; verb(s) must be present, e.g. *Mi programa favorita es/se llama EastEnders. Lo veo/Lo ponen el domingo a las dos.*
b)		**One** detail only, however basic	**Two** clear details required **without** verb(s), e.g. *Telenovela en centro de Londres.*	**Two** clear details **with** verb(s)	**Two** clear details **with** verb(s), e.g. *Es una telenovela. Trata de unas familias (que viven) en Londres.*
c)		Name + **one** detail only	Name of person + **three** details **without** verb(s) Name + **two** details	Name of person + **three** details **with** verb(s)	Name of person + **three** details **with** verb(s), e.g. *Se llama Alfie. Trabaja en el pub, tiene los ojos azules y es gracioso.*
d)		**One** reason only	Appropriate response **without** verb(s) and **two** reasons	Appropriate response **with** verb(s) and **two** reasons	Appropriate response **with** verb(s) and **two** reasons (may be same as in **b)** above), e.g. *La historia es interesante (y) hay mucha acción.*

CANDIDATE'S ROLE

> You are discussing radio and television with your Spanish friend.
>
> a) • *Tu preferencia entre la radio y la televisión y tu razón.*
> b) • *Tu opinión sobre los anuncios y tu razón.*
> c) • *Tu programa favorito y descripción (**dos** detalles).*
> d) • ▐
>
> When you see ▐ you will have to respond to something which you have not prepared. Your teacher will play the part of your friend and will speak first.

■ TO HELP YOU

a) This task invites you to state your preference between radio and television, but it's the reason that is important. Use the first person singular of *preferir* and go on to explain that you like to 'listen to' or 'watch' certain types of programmes, for example. Try to keep your answer fairly general and leave something for the third task!

b) There are advertisements on both radio and TV, so you can perhaps start by saying you like them or not and then give a reason: maybe you think they're good/fun/necessary/important, or perhaps you think they're bad/stupid/noisy/boring. Remember that you'll have to make your adjectives agree with the word ('advertisements') they describe.

c) This is an opportunity to mention one programme by name and give two details about it, e.g. day/time you watch it; what it's about (story/action/location); describe who takes part in it. 'My favourite programme is/is called ...' (and just give its name in English). 'I watch it/they show it on (day) at (time)', etc.

d) This is the unpredictable task! After talking a lot about these free time activities, what might the conversation move on to, perhaps?

■ JOT DOWN YOUR ANSWERS

a) _____

b) _____

c) _____

d) _____

TEACHER'S ROLE

1 Introduce the situation and then ask whether the candidate prefers radio or television and why.
Estás hablando con tu amigo español/tu amiga española. Yo soy tu amigo/amiga.
¿Prefieres la radio o la televisión? . . . ¿Por qué?

2 Allow the candidate to say if he/she prefers radio or television and to give a reason.
Ask the candidate's opinion of advertisements and why.
¿Cuál es tu opinión sobre los anuncios? . . . ¿Por qué?

3 Allow the candidate to give his/her opinion of advertisements and to say why.
Ask the candidate which programme he/she prefers and to describe it. Elicit **two** details.

¿Cuál es tu programa favorito? . . . Describe programa.

4 🔳 Allow the candidate to say what programme he/she prefers and to give **two** details.
Ask what other things young people do in his/her country. Elicit **two** details.
¿Qué otras actividades hacen los jóvenes en tu país?

5 Allow the candidate to give **two** other activities that young people do in his/her country.
End the conversation by saying that seems fun.
Parece divertido.

■ MARK SCHEME

	0	1	2	3	4
	Message not communicated	Appropriate response/ difficulty or ambiguity/ some relevant information	Appropriate and unambiguous/minor errors or minor omissions	Appropriate and full response/minor errors cause no ambiguity/ TWO minor errors max.	Appropriate and correct response/task fully accomplished/NO SIGNIFICANT ERROR/ ONE minor error max.
a)		Opinion with no reason	Preference plus reason **without** verb(s)	Preference plus reason **with** verb(s)	Preference for TV/ radio with reason; verb(s) essential, e.g. *Prefiero la radio (porque) ponen muchos programas de música.*
b)		Opinion on its own	Opinion + reason **without** verb(s), e.g. *Anuncios horribles – muy estúpidos.*	Opinion + reason **with** verb(s)	Opinion + reason; verb(s) essential, e.g. *Me gustan mucho (los anuncios) (porque) son divertidos.*
c)		**One** detail only 'Prefiere(s)' + **two** details One detail without verb(s)	**Two** details **without** verb(s) e.g. *Programa favorito Top of the Pops – mucha música y grupos estupendos.*	**Two** details **with** verb(s)	**Two** details; verb(s) essential, e.g. *Prefiero 'The Bill'. Trata de una comisaría en Londres. Hay mucha acción.*
d)		Only **one** activity	**Two** activities **without** verb(s) Verb(s) in first person **singular**	**Two** activities (as in 4 mark column)	**Two** activities, in either first or third person **plural** of verb(s), e.g. *Practican deportes y van a la discoteca.* Accept *Se puede.*

CANDIDATE'S ROLE

> You are in Spain. You telephone the ticket office of the bullring to find out when the next bullfight is and how long it lasts.
>
> **a)**   • *Razón por tu llamada.*
> **b)**   • *Reserva para ti y tu familia y situación en la plaza de toros.*
> **c)**   • *Forma de pago, tu apellido y cómo se escribe.*
> **d)**   • **!**
>
> When you see **!** you will have to respond to something which you have not prepared. Your teacher will play the part of the ticket seller and will speak first.

■ TO HELP YOU

a) The rubric gives you everything you need to know to carry out the first task: 'When is the next bullfight and how long does it last?' If you don't want to use the question word 'when?' ask 'what day?' The question word 'how long?' doesn't use the word 'long'! Try saying 'how much time?' or 'how many hours?' Remember that 'does' is not part of the Spanish question: just use the third person singular of the verb 'to last'.

b) This task involves buying tickets for you and your family somewhere in the bullring. They often sell seats 'in the sun' or 'in the shade', but you can ask for seats 'near the centre', 'at the back', 'beside the entrance' or something like that. To say 'I want ...' or 'I would like ...' use the verb *querer* (present tense, or special form of the conditional) or *gustar* (conditional tense).

c) There are three parts to this task. You could pay in 'euros' or 'traveller's cheques', for example. When you give your name, make sure it's your surname that you spell!

d) This is the unpredictable task! Have you ever been to a bullfight? They don't have them in this country, so what might the ticket seller end the conversation by asking?

JOT DOWN YOUR ANSWERS

a) _____

b) _____

c) _____

d) _____

TEACHER'S ROLE

1 Introduce the situation and then answer the telephone.
Hablas por teléfono con el taquillero/la taquillera de la plaza de toros. Yo soy el taquillero/la taquillera. ¡Dígame!

2 Allow the candidate to ask when the next bullfight is and how long it lasts.
Say it is on Sunday the 16th and lasts three hours.
Es el domingo, día 16. Dura tres horas en total.

3 Allow the candidate to book tickets for himself/herself and his/her family, and to say where he/she would like the seats.
Ask how he/she is going to pay. Ask for his/her name and the spelling of his/her surname.

¿Cómo va a pagar? . . . ¿Cómo se llama usted? . . . ¿Cómo se escribe su apellido?

4 ❗ Allow the candidate to say how he/she is going to pay, to give his/her name and to spell the surname. Ask the candidate what opinions people in his/her country have of bullfighting. Elicit **two** opinions.
¿Qué opina la gente de su país sobre las corridas de toros?

5 Allow the candidate to give **two** opinions that people have of bullfighting.
End the conversation by saying that you hope the candidate enjoys the bullfight.
Espero que le guste la corrida.

■ MARK SCHEME

	0	1	2	3	4
	Message not communicated	Appropriate response/ difficulty or ambiguity/ some relevant information	Appropriate and unambiguous/minor errors or minor omissions	Appropriate and full response/minor errors cause no ambiguity/ TWO minor errors max.	Appropriate and correct response/task fully accomplished/NO SIGNIFICANT ERROR/ ONE minor error max.
a)		One element only	Full response **without** verbs	As in 4 marks column	Both questions, e.g. *¿Cuándo/Qué día es la próxima corrida (de toros) (y) cuánto tiempo/cuántas horas dura?*
b)		*Quisiera reservar para mi familia* + position		Full response as in 4 marks column	Number of tickets required + place in bullring, e.g. *Quiero cuatro entradas cerca de la entrada (por favor).*
c)		**One** element only	**Two** elements only	**Three** elements	**Three** elements; verb(s) <u>not</u> essential if responding to teacher prompts
d)	English pronunciation of 'cruel'	**One** opinion only	**Two** opinions **without** verb(s)	**Two** opinions	**Two** opinions needed, e.g. *Es cruel y peligroso./No le gusta nada.*

CANDIDATE'S ROLE

Your Spanish friend is staying with you. Your friend would like to go to the cinema, but they are showing a film you have already seen.

a) • *Tu problema.*
b) • *Tu opinión de la película y tu razón.*
c) • *Descripción de la película (**dos** detalles).*
d) • **!**

When you see **!** you will have to respond to something which you have not prepared. Your teacher will play the part of your friend and will speak first.

■ TO HELP YOU

a) This task requires you to say: 'They are showing a film that I've already seen.' There are two verbs for 'to show' in Spanish: *mostrar* (to indicate, demonstrate) and *poner* (to put on). Which one will you use? Use the perfect tense of the verb 'to see' and to join both halves of the sentence together use *que* for 'that'. Where are you going to put the word for 'already'?

b) Your opinion can be positive or negative, but you need to give a reason. You don't have to name the film, but you could comment on the actors, the length, the photography, the music, etc. You can use the present tense. Make sure you leave something to say for the next task!

c) This task really requires you to say what the film is about – well, enough to get a few marks, anyway! Use the classic Spanish phrase for 'it's about . . .' or 'it's the story of . . .' and mention, for example, what kind of film it is, a key element of the plot, where it takes place, how it ends, whether it's a happy or a sad story, or things like that. Not too much, but not too little.

d) This is the unpredictable task! From the information given it sounds as if you don't want to see the film again, so what might your friend ask? Remember to offer a reason, too.

■ JOT DOWN YOUR ANSWERS

a) _____

b) _____

c) _____

d) _____

ROLE PLAY 21   A FILM YOU'VE ALREADY SEEN

ROLE PLAY 21

TEACHER'S ROLE

1 Begin the conversation by setting the scene and suggesting you go to the cinema this evening.
Estás en casa con tu amigo español/tu amiga española. Yo soy tu amigo/amiga.
¿Por qué no vamos al cine esta tarde?

2 Allow the candidate to say they are showing a film he/she has already seen.
Ask the candidate what he/she thinks of the film and why.
¿Qué tal la película? . . . ¿Por qué?

3 Allow the candidate to say what he/she thinks of the film and why.

Ask the candidate what the film is about. Elicit **two** details.
¿De qué trata la película?

4 ❗ Allow the candidate to give **two** details of what the film is about.
Ask the candidate what he/she wants to do instead. Elicit a reason.
Pues, ¿qué otra cosa quieres hacer? . . . ¿Por qué?

5 Allow the candidate to say what he/she wants to do instead and why.
End the conversation by agreeing to the suggestion.
De acuerdo.

MARK SCHEME

	0	1	2	3	4
	Message not communicated	Appropriate response/ difficulty or ambiguity/ some relevant information	Appropriate and unambiguous/minor errors or minor omissions	Appropriate and full response/minor errors cause no ambiguity/ TWO minor errors max.	Appropriate and correct response/task fully accomplished/NO SIGNIFICANT ERROR/ ONE minor error max.
a)		Partial response causing ambiguity	Omission of 'already'	Full response	Full and correct response, e.g. *Ponen una película que ya he visto.*
b)	Reason alone	Opinion only	Opinion and reason **without** verb(s)	Opinion and reason **with** verb(s)	Opinion and reason **with** verb(s), e.g. *Es fenomenal (porque) los actores son muy buenos.*
c)		**One** detail only	Full response with **two** details but **without** verb(s)	Full response with **two** details and verb(s)	**Two** details required with verb(s), e.g. *Es la historia de una familia (y) trata de sus problemas con la policía.* Accept type of film
d)		Omission of reason	Activity plus reason **without** verb(s), e.g. *Bolera porque fenomenal.*	Activity plus reason **with** verb(s)	Alternative activity and reason, e.g. *(Podemos) ir a la bolera (porque) mis amigos van (allí) (esta noche).* Infinitive OK

ROLE PLAY 22

CANDIDATE'S ROLE

Your Spanish friend is staying at your house. Your friend suggests going to a club, but you do not want to because there are lots of problems there every night.

a) • *Tu razón para no ir al club.*

b) • ***Dos** detalles de los problemas.*

c) • *Otras **dos** actividades para esta noche.*

d) • ❗

When you see ❗ you will have to respond to something which you have not prepared. Your teacher will play the part of your friend and will speak first.

■ TO HELP YOU

a) You could start this task by saying you don't want to go to the club, but the main thing is to say that there are problems there every night. Use the first person singular of *querer*, make it negative and then use the infinitive 'to go'. There are two ways to say 'every night' – one is singular and the other is plural. If you're not sure how to say 'there', say 'at the club'.

b) This task asks you to mention **two** details about the problems. You could either say two things about one problem, or talk about two different problems. Perhaps some people drink too much, smoke too much, have fights, take drugs, or things like that. You could count these (few) people so use *algunas personas* rather than *la gente* (which might mean all of them), and use the third person plural of your verbs.

c) Since going to the club has been ruled out, you're asked to suggest **two** other things you could do this evening. Perhaps you could begin by saying: 'Let's …' or 'We can …' or 'Do you want to …?' Remember that the second verb will be in the infinitive!

d) This is the unpredictable task! Having just been asked to suggest **two** different activities, what might your friend ask next? Always be prepared to give a reason!

■ JOT DOWN YOUR ANSWERS

a) _____

b) _____

c) _____

d) _____

TEACHER'S ROLE

1 Introduce the situation, then ask the candidate why he/she does not want to go to the club.
Estás hablando con tu amigo español/tu amiga española. Yo soy tu amigo/amiga.
¿Por qué no quieres ir al club?

2 Allow the candidate to say there are lots of problems at the club every night.
Ask what the problems are. Elicit **two** details.
¿Qué problemas hay?

3 Allow the candidate to give **two** problems, or **two** details about one problem.

Ask what else you can do. Elicit **two** activities.
Bueno. ¿Qué otras cosas podemos hacer?

4 ❗ Allow the candidate to suggest **two** other activities.
Ask the candidate which of these activities he/she prefers and why.
¿Cuál de estas actividades prefieres tú? . . . ¿Por qué?

5 Allow the candidate to say which activity he/she prefers and to say why.
End the conversation by agreeing to the suggestion.
De acuerdo.

■ MARK SCHEME

	0	1	2	3	4
	Message not communicated	Appropriate response/ difficulty or ambiguity/ some relevant information	Appropriate and unambiguous/minor errors or minor omissions	Appropriate and full response/minor errors cause no ambiguity/ TWO minor errors max.	Appropriate and correct response/task fully accomplished/NO SIGNIFICANT ERROR/ ONE minor error max.
a)		Omission of *cada noche/ todas las noches*	Full response **without** verb(s), e.g. *Problemas cada noche.*	Full response **with** verb(s)	Full and correct response, e.g. *Hay problemas (en el club) cada noche/todas las noches.*
b)		**One** problem only, e.g. *Drogas.*	**Two** problems **without** verb(s), e.g. *Drogas y alcohol.*	**Two** problems **with** verb(s)	**Two** problems **with** verb(s), e.g. *(Algunas personas) beben demasiado y toman drogas.*
c)		**One** activity only	**Two** activities **without** verb(s), e.g. *Cine o bolera.*	**Two** activities **with** verb(s)	**Two** activities (infinitives or invitation OK), e.g. *Vamos a . . ./¿Quieres . . .?/Podemos . . . ir al cine o jugar con el ordenador.*
d)		Preferred activity only Reason only	Preferred activity plus reason **without** verb(s)	Preferred activity plus reason **with** verb(s)	Preferred activity plus reason **with** verb(s), e.g. *(Prefiero) ir al cine (porque) ponen una buena película.*

CANDIDATE'S ROLE

> It is the **last** day of your holiday in Spain. You have bought a jumper, but there is a problem with it. You take it back to the shop.
>
> **a)** • *Detalles de la compra – qué y cuándo.*
> **b)** • *Descripción exacta del problema.*
> **c)** • *Tu sugerencia para resolver el problema.*
> **d)** • **!**
>
> When you see **!** you will have to respond to something which you have not prepared. Your teacher will play the part of the shop assistant and will speak first.

■ TO HELP YOU

a) In this task you need to explain to the assistant: 'I bought this jumper (here) . . .' and say when. You will need the first person singular of the preterite tense of the verb 'to buy', which is perfectly regular. Suggest a time like 'this morning' or 'yesterday', perhaps.

b) Now you need to say what exactly the nature of the problem is. A one word answer such as 'dirty' is not likely to gain many marks, so be a bit more adventurous, use a verb and give a couple of details, perhaps saying it's too big/tight, or there's a small hole in it, or your friend doesn't like the colour, for example.

c) This is your opportunity to say what you want to do. Perhaps you want a bigger/smaller jumper, or one in a different colour. Or maybe you just want to change it, or ask for your money back. It will depend a bit on what you said in the previous task.

d) This is the unpredictable task! If you look back at the rubric you will notice that one key piece of information doesn't appear to have been taken into account. If it is the **last** day of your holiday, what do you think the assistant might suggest? And how could you reply?

■ JOT DOWN YOUR ANSWERS

a) _____

b) _____

c) _____

d) _____

TEACHER'S ROLE

1 Begin the conversation by explaining the situation and then greet the candidate and ask him/her how you can help.
Estamos en una tienda de ropa en España. Yo soy el dependiente/la dependienta.
¡Hola! Buenos días. ¿Qué desea?

2 Allow the candidate to explain what he/she has bought and when he/she bought it.
Ask how you can help.
Bien. ¿En qué puedo ayudarle?

3 Allow the candidate to describe exactly what is wrong with the jumper.
Ask the candidate what he/she wants to do about it?
Bueno, ¿qué quiere hacer?

4 ⚠ Allow the candidate to say what he/she wants to do about it.

Tell him/her that it is not possible to do that. Tell him/her that in three days there will be more jumpers available. Ask if he/she can wait till then, and when the candidate says he/she cannot, ask him/her why not.
Pues, no es posible. Lo siento. Pero recibiremos muchos otros jerseys dentro de tres días.
¿Puede esperar y volver dentro de tres días? . . . ¿Por qué no?

5 Allow the candidate to explain that he/she cannot return later as he/she is due to return home tomorrow. End the conversation by agreeing to give him/her the money back.
Ah, entiendo. Entonces le devuelvo el dinero.

■ MARK SCHEME

	0	1	2	3	4
	Message not communicated	Appropriate response/ difficulty or ambiguity/ some relevant information	Appropriate and unambiguous/minor errors or minor omissions	Appropriate and full response/minor errors cause no ambiguity/ TWO minor errors max.	Appropriate and correct response/task fully accomplished/NO SIGNIFICANT ERROR/ ONE minor error max.
a)	*Tengo problema.* *Jersey* (on its own) Wrong garment	Wrong person of verb	Full response **without** verb(s)	Clear idea of jumper bought and when **with** verb(s)	Clear idea of jumper bought and when; verb(s) must be used, e.g. *Compré el/este jersey (aquí) esta mañana/ayer.*
b)			Appropriate response **without** verb(s)	Appropriate response **with** verb(s)	Appropriate response – clearly expressed problem, with verb(s), e.g. *Es demasiado pequeño./Tiene un pequeño agujero.*
c)		Response causing ambiguity, e.g. *Dinero por favor.*	Appropriate response **without** verb(s)	Appropriate response **with** verb(s)	Appropriate response **with** verb(s), e.g. *¿Puedo cambiarlo por otro?/Quiero un reembolso (por favor).*
d)	Positive response	Response only, e.g. *No* (on its own).	Negative response plus reason **without** verb(s)	Negative response plus reason **with** verb(s)	Negative response plus reason **with** verb(s), e.g. *No (es posible) (porque) hoy es mi último día en España.*

CANDIDATE'S ROLE

> You and your friends are camping in Spain. Unfortunately you are having problems with the family in the next tent. You go to reception to complain about the family.
>
> **a)** • *Tu problema.*
> **b)** • ***Dos*** *detalles del problema con la familia.*
> **c)** • *Tu sugerencia para resolver el problema.*
> **d)** • **!**
>
> When you see **!** you will have to respond to something which you have not prepared. Your teacher will play the part of the receptionist and will speak first.

■ TO HELP YOU

a) The rubric guides you to tell the receptionist: 'I/We have a problem with the family in the next tent.' The present tense of *tener* will be fine, but there are different ways of saying 'next': *próximo* (next, following, coming) or *al lado* (next, beside). Which one would be best here?

b) Use your imagination to give **two** details of the problem with the family, but keep your information fairly simple. Perhaps they make a lot of noise during the evening, or throw rubbish on the ground by your tent, or something like that. Use the third person singular of your verbs if you refer to 'the family', or the third person plural if you just say 'they'.

c) This is your opportunity to suggest a solution. Perhaps you would like to change the place you have, or you want a reduction in the cost of your place, or you would like some rubbish bins by their tent, or something like that.

d) This is the unpredictable task! Notice that you are speaking to the receptionist about the problem. What might he/she ask you about what you have or haven't done?

■ JOT DOWN YOUR ANSWERS

a) _____

b) _____

c) _____

d) _____

ROLE PLAY 24

TEACHER'S ROLE

1 Begin the conversation by setting the scene and asking the candidate how you can help.
Estás en un camping en España. Yo soy el recepcionista/la recepcionista.
¿En qué puedo ayudarle?

2 Allow the candidate to complain about the family in the next tent. Ask the candidate what exactly the family is doing. Elicit **two** details.
¿Qué hace la familia exactamente?

3 Allow the candidate to give **two** details about the family's behaviour.
Ask what the candidate wants to do about it.
¿Qué quiere hacer?

4 ⚠ Allow the candidate to say what he/she wants to do to resolve the problem.

Reject the candidate's suggestion. Ask the candidate if he/she has spoken to the family about the problem.
If **yes** – elicit the reaction of the family.
If **no** – elicit a reason for not speaking to the family.
Eso no. ¿Ha hablado usted con la familia del problema?
¿Cómo reaccionaron?/¿Por qué no?

5 Allow the candidate to say what the reaction of the family was, or give a reason for not speaking to the family.
End the conversation by saying you will speak to the family yourself.
No se preocupe. Hablaré con la familia.

■ MARK SCHEME

	0	1	2	3	4
	Message not communicated	Appropriate response/ difficulty or ambiguity/ some relevant information	Appropriate and unambiguous/minor errors or minor omissions	Appropriate and full response/minor errors cause no ambiguity/ TWO minor errors max.	Appropriate and correct response/task fully accomplished/NO SIGNIFICANT ERROR/ ONE minor error max.
a)		Partial response, e.g. *Problema con familia.*	Appropriate response **without** verb(s) e.g. *Problema con la familia al lado.*	Full response **with** verb(s)	Full response **with** verbs, e.g. *Hay un problema con la familia de la tienda de al lado.*
b)	Inappropriate response, e.g. *Hay cuatro personas.*	One detail only	Two clear details **without** verbs, e.g. *Ruido y basura.*	**Two** appropriate details of the problem **with** verb(s)	**Two** appropriate details of the problem with the family, **with** verb(s), e.g. *Hacen mucho ruido hasta las tres de la madrugada.*
c)			Appropriate response **without** verb(s), e.g. *Otro sitio.*	Appropriate response **with** verb(s)	Appropriate response **with** verb(s), e.g. *(Quiero) cambiar de sitio.*
d)		*No/Sí* alone *No/Sí* + repeated information	*No/Sí* + added information **without** verb(s)	Appropriate response (as in 4 marks column) **with** verb(s)	Appropriate response **with** verb(s), *No/Sí* + further detail (but **without** repetition of earlier problem), e.g. **Sí** . . . *pero no hacen nada/se enfadan mucho;* **No** . . . *porque no hablan inglés o español.*

CANDIDATE'S ROLE

> You are having a meal with your family in a restaurant in Spain.
> Unfortunately, you are not very happy about the waiter. You speak to
> the owner of the restaurant to complain.
>
> **a)** • *Tu problema.*
> **b)** • ***Dos*** *detalles del problema.*
> **c)** • ❗
> **d)** • *Tu sugerencia para resolver el problema.*
>
> When you see ❗ you will have to respond to something which you
> have not prepared. Your teacher will play the part of the restaurant
> owner and will speak first.

■ TO HELP YOU

a) Following the guidance of the rubric, you simply have to say that you are not very happy with the waiter. There are two verbs for 'to be' in Spanish: *ser* (for permanent characteristics) and *estar* (for temporary feelings). Which one do you need here? Use the first person singular.

b) Use your imagination to give **two** details of the problems with the waiter, but keep your information fairly simple. Perhaps he serves the food very slowly, or he has dirty hands, or he speaks too fast, or something like that. Use the third person singular of your verb(s) to talk about him.

c) This is the unpredictable task! What other useful information might the owner of the restaurant want to know?

d) Now you have the opportunity to resolve the problem. Perhaps you would like a different waiter, or a discount, or a free dessert/drink, or something like that. Remember they say that the customer is always right!

■ JOT DOWN YOUR ANSWERS

a) _____

b) _____

c) _____

d) _____

TEACHER'S ROLE

1   Introduce the situation, then ask the candidate how you can help.
Estamos en un restaurante en España. Yo soy el dueño/la dueña.
¿En qué puedo ayudarle?

2   Allow the candidate to complain about the waiter.
Apologise and ask what the problem is. Elicit **two** details.
Lo siento. ¿Cuál es el problema exactamente?

3   ■ Allow the candidate to give **two** details about the problem.
Tell the candidate that you need to speak to the waiter. Ask the
candidate to describe the waiter. Elicit **three** details.
Necesito hablar con el camarero. Describa a su camarero, por favor.

4   Allow the candidate to give **three** details about the waiter.
Say you will talk to the waiter. Ask what you can do to resolve the problem.
Bien. Hablaré con el camarero. ¿Qué podemos hacer para resolver
el problema?

5   Allow the candidate to suggest a solution.
End the conversation by accepting the candidate's solution and by
apologising.
De acuerdo. Lo siento.

■ MARK SCHEME

	0	1	2	3	4
	Message not communicated	Appropriate response/ difficulty or ambiguity/ some relevant information	Appropriate and unambiguous/minor errors or minor omissions	Appropriate and full response/minor errors cause no ambiguity/ TWO minor errors max.	Appropriate and correct response/task fully accomplished/NO SIGNIFICANT ERROR/ ONE minor error max.
a)	*Camarero* on its own		Clear complaint about the waiter **without** verb(s)	Clear complaint about the waiter **with** verb(s)	Clear complaint about the waiter **with** verb(s), e.g. *No estoy contento/a con el camarero.*
b)		One detail only	Clear reference to **two** details **without** verb(s)	Clear reference to **two** details **with** verb(s)	Clear reference to **two** details; verb(s) essential, e.g. *¡Sirve la comida lentamente y habla rápidamente!*
c)		One detail only	**Three** clear details about the waiter **without** verb(s) **Two** details **with** verb(s)	**Three** clear details about the waiter **with** verb(s)	**Three** clear details about the waiter **with** verb(s), e.g. *Es alto, tiene el pelo negro y lleva gafas.*
d)			Appropriate response **without** verb(s), e.g. *Camarero diferente.*	Appropriate response **with** verb(s)	Appropriate response **with** verb(s), e.g. *Quiero un postre gratis/un descuento de un diez por ciento.*

ROLE PLAY 26

CANDIDATE'S ROLE

You are on holiday in Spain and you have been on a coach trip. Unfortunately you are not very happy with the guide. You telephone the manager of the coach company to complain.

a) • *Tu problema.*

b) • ***Dos*** *detalles del problema.*

c) • **!**

d) • *Tu sugerencia para resolver el problema.*

When you see **!** you will have to respond to something which you have not prepared. Your teacher will play the part of the manager and will speak first.

■ TO HELP YOU

a) Explain to the manager of the coach company that you are not very happy with the guide. Leave the actual details of the problem till the next task. As an alternative to saying 'I'm not happy with ...' you could say 'I want to complain about ...' using *querer* followed by the infinitive of the reflexive verb *quejarse*. How will you change the *se* at the end of the infinitive?

b) There are lots of possible complaints that you might have. Perhaps the guide speaks too fast, or doesn't answer your questions, or smokes in the coach, or something like that. Use the third person singular of the verb(s) you choose.

c) This is the unpredictable task! What other useful information might the manager want to know?

d) Now you have the opportunity to resolve the problem. Perhaps you would like a discount for another coach trip, or your money back, or a letter from the guide saying sorry, or something like that.

■ JOT DOWN YOUR ANSWERS

a) _____

b) _____

c) _____

d) _____

TEACHER'S ROLE

1 Introduce the situation, then answer the telephone.
Estás hablando por teléfono con el director/la directora de una compañía de autocares en España. Yo soy el director/la directora.
¡Dígame! ¿En qué puedo ayudarle?

2 Allow the candidate to explain that he/she has had a problem with the guide.
Apologise and ask what the problem is. Elicit **two** details.
Lo siento. ¿Cuál es el problema exactamente?

3 ▮ Allow the candidate to give **two** details about the problem.
Ask for a description of the guide. Elicit **three** details.

Necesito hablar con el guía. Describe a su guía por favor.

4 Allow the candidate to give **three** details about the guide.
Say you will talk to the guide. Ask what you can do to resolve the problem.
Pues, hablaré con el guía. ¿Qué podemos hacer para resolver el problema?

5 Allow the candidate to suggest a solution.
End the conversation by accepting the candidate's solution and by apologising.
De acuerdo. Lo siento mucho.

■ MARK SCHEME

	0	1	2	3	4
	Message not communicated	Appropriate response/ difficulty or ambiguity/ some relevant information	Appropriate and unambiguous/minor errors or minor omissions	Appropriate and full response/minor errors cause no ambiguity/ TWO minor errors max.	Appropriate and correct response/task fully accomplished/NO SIGNIFICANT ERROR/ ONE minor error max.
a)		*Tengo (un) problema* (on its own)	Clear complaint about the guide **without** verb(s) Omission of any reference to excursion/coach	Clear complaint about the guide **with** verb(s)	Clear complaint about the guide **with** verb(s), e.g. *Había un problema con el guía en la excursión. Quiero quejarme del guía del autocar.*
b)		One detail only	Clear reference to **two** details **without** verb(s)	Clear reference to **two** details **with** verb(s)	Clear reference to **two** details; verb(s) essential, e.g. *Habla demasiado rápidamente a los turistas.*
c)		One detail only	**Three** clear details about the guide **without** verb(s) **Two** details **with** verb(s)	**Three** clear details about the guide **with** verb(s)	**Three** clear details about the guide **with** verb(s), e.g. *Es moreno/a, tiene los ojos marrones y habla con (un) acento portugués.*
d)			Appropriate response **without** verb(s), e.g. *Guía diferente.*	Appropriate response **with** verb(s)	Appropriate response **with** verb(s), e.g. *Quisiera un reembolso/un descuento de un diez por ciento para otra excursión.*

ROLE PLAY **27**

CANDIDATE'S ROLE

You are talking with your Spanish friend about your future studies and career.

a) • *Tus estudios en el futuro y tu razón.*
b) • **Dos** *inconvenientes de más estudios.*
c) • *Tu trabajo ideal (**dos** detalles).*
d) • !

When you see ! you will have to respond to something which you have not prepared. Your teacher will play the part of your friend and will speak first.

■ TO HELP YOU

a) The first task invites you to talk about your studies in the future and why. Perhaps you are going to go to college or university to study (any subject) because you want to become (any profession). Or maybe you're not going to study in the future because you want to get a job. Use the verbs *ir a* (plus infinitive) for 'I'm going to ...', and *querer* (plus infinitive) for 'want to ...'.

b) Whether you're going on to study or not, I'm sure you can think of some disadvantages of doing more studying in the future! Perhaps you've done enough exams! Or you won't earn money, or you won't have much free time. Be sure to give **two** disadvantages, but keep them fairly simple. You could use present or future tenses.

c) Regardless of your studies, and even if you've mentioned a profession in the first task, give **two** details of your ideal job. Perhaps you could use a future or a conditional tense. Perhaps you would work with people, travel abroad, earn a lot of money, have a fast car, be boss of a big team, or that sort of thing.

d) This is the unpredictable task! Given that this role play is focusing very much on the future, what else might your friend ask?

■ JOT DOWN YOUR ANSWERS

a) _____

b) _____

c) _____

d) _____

53

TEACHER'S ROLE

1 Introduce the situation, then ask the candidate what his/her plans are for his/her future studies and to give a reason.
Estamos hablando de los estudios. Yo soy tu amigo español/tu amiga española.
Háblame un poco de tus estudios futuros. . . . ¿Por qué dices eso?

2 Allow the candidate to talk about his/her future studies (if any) and to give a reason.
Ask the candidate what disadvantages there are to further studies. Elicit **two** disadvantages.
En tu opinión, ¿cuáles son los inconvenientes de seguir estudiando?

3 Allow the candidate to give **two** disadvantages of further studies.

Ask the candidate what his/her ideal job would be like. Elicit **two** details.
¿Y cómo sería tu trabajo ideal?

4 ❗ Allow the candidate to give **two** details about his/her ideal job.
Ask the candidate what other plans he/she has for the future. Elicit **two** details.
¿Qué otros planes tienes para el futuro?

5 Allow the candidate to give **two** details of other plans he/she has for the future.
End the conversation by saying that you want to get married.
Yo quiero casarme.

■ MARK SCHEME

	0	1	2	3	4
	Message not communicated	Appropriate response/ difficulty or ambiguity/ some relevant information	Appropriate and unambiguous/minor errors or minor omissions	Appropriate and full response/minor errors cause no ambiguity/ TWO minor errors max.	Appropriate and correct response/task fully accomplished/NO SIGNIFICANT ERROR/ ONE minor error max.
a)		Omission of reason	Statement and reason **without** verb(s), e.g. *universidad – buena carrera.*	Statement and reason **with** verb(s)	Statement about future studies and reason **with** verb(s), e.g. *Voy a ir a la universidad (porque) quiero ser médico.*
b)		**One** disadvantage only	**Two** clear disadvantages **without** verb(s)	**Two** clear disadvantages **with** verb(s)	**Two** clear disadvantages **with** verb(s), e.g. *Hay muchos exámenes y no ganas dinero.*
c)		**One** detail only	**Two** clear details of ideal job **without** verb(s)	**Two** clear details of ideal job **with** verb(s)	**Two** clear details of ideal job **with** verb(s), e.g. *Trabajaría con la gente y viajaría mucho.*
d)		**One** detail only	Appropriate response **without** verb(s)	Appropriate response **with** verb(s)	Appropriate response **with** verb(s) and **two** details, e.g. *Voy a visitar a mi amigo/a español(a)./Quiero casarme y tener una familia.*

CANDIDATE'S ROLE

> You are discussing work with your Spanish friend.
>
> **a)** • *Tu trabajo futuro y **dos** razones.*
> **b)** • ***Dos** inconvenientes de este trabajo.*
> **c)** • ▉
> **d)** • *Tu opinión sobre trabajar en el extranjero y **dos** razones.*
>
> When you see ▉ you will have to respond to something which you have not prepared. Your teacher will play the part of your friend and will speak first.

■ TO HELP YOU

a) For this task you will need to state what job you'd like in the future and give **two** reasons. You could start with the conditional tense of *gustar*, for example, followed by the infinitive of the verb 'to be' (will it be *ser* or *estar*?). There could be many reasons, but you might want to mention place, hours, salary, holidays, colleagues, travel, etc. Try to keep the language fairly straightforward.

b) No job is perfect, so there are bound to be disadvantages. Try **not** to contradict what you've said in the previous task, but you could mention any of the above things – this time in a negative way. Again you could use the conditional tense, of *tener que* ('to have to'), or *gustar*, followed by the infinitive.

c) This is the unpredictable task! Within the context of your future career plans, what or who might your friend ask you about?

d) Now you need to give an opinion about working abroad and **two** reasons. The opinion could be a simple yes (I would like it) or no (I wouldn't like it), but the reasons will be important. Perhaps you could consider such things as experience, climate, language, salary, travel, family, friends, health, cost of living, etc., but keep your language simple.

■ JOT DOWN YOUR ANSWERS

a) _____

b) _____

c) _____

d) _____

ROLE PLAY 28

TEACHER'S ROLE

1 Introduce the situation and then ask the candidate what type of job he/she would like to do in the future and why. Elicit a specific occupation and **two** reasons.
Estás hablando con tu amigo español/tu amiga española. Yo soy tu amigo/amiga.
¿Qué tipo de trabajo te gustaría hacer en el futuro? . . . ¿Por qué?

2 Allow the candidate to say what job he/she would like to do in the future and give **two** reasons why. Ask the candidate what the disadvantages of this job are. Elicit **two** disadvantages.
¿Cuáles son los inconvenientes de este trabajo?

3 ⚠ Allow the candidate to give **two** disadvantages of this job.

Ask what his/her parents think of these plans.
¿Qué opinan tus padres sobre tus planes?

4 Allow the candidate to say what his/her parents think of these plans.
Ask the candidate whether he/she would like to work abroad and why (not). Elicit **two** reasons.
¿Te gustaría trabajar en el extranjero? . . . ¿Por qué (no)?

5 Allow the candidate to say whether or not he/she would like to work abroad and to give **two** reasons why (not).
End the conversation by agreeing with the candidate.
Sí. Estoy de acuerdo.

■ MARK SCHEME

	0	1	2	3	4
	Message not communicated	Appropriate response/ difficulty or ambiguity/ some relevant information	Appropriate and unambiguous/minor errors or minor omissions	Appropriate and full response/minor errors cause no ambiguity/ TWO minor errors max.	Appropriate and correct response/task fully accomplished/NO SIGNIFICANT ERROR/ ONE minor error max.
a)		**One** reason only	Future job with **two** reasons and **without** verb(s) *Me gusta* + rest OK.	Future job with **two** reasons and **with** verb(s)	Future job with **two** reasons and **with** verb(s), e.g. *Me gustaría ser piloto (porque) viajaría y ganaría mucho dinero.*
b)		**One** disadvantage only	**Two** clear disadvantages **without** verb(s)	**Two** clear disadvantages **with** verb(s)	**Two** disadvantages **with** verb(s), e.g. *No me gustarían las horas de trabajo. Tendría que llevar un uniforme horrible.*
c)		Appropriate response with errors causing ambiguity, e.g. first/ second person of verb(s)	Omission of *mi padre/ madre* in front of third person singular	As in 4 marks column	Third person plural of verb with *mis padres*, or use of third person singular **with** *mi madre* or *mi padre*, e.g. *Mi(s) padre(s) piensa(n) que es una buena idea.*
d)		Response only, e.g. *Sí/ No.* **One** reason only	Appropriate response **Two** reasons **without** verb(s)	Response plus **two** reasons	Response + **two** reasons, e.g. *Sí (porque) sería una buena experiencia, y aprendería más idiomas.* Accept *me gusta(ría)*

CANDIDATE'S ROLE

> You are staying with a Spanish family. One night you get in very late and the family has been worried.
>
> **a)** • *Tu explicación por llegar tarde.*
> **b)** • !
> **c)** • *Reacción de tus padres si llegas tarde a casa.*
> **d)** • *Dos actividades para mañana.*
>
> When you see ! you will have to respond to something which you have not prepared. Your teacher will play the part of the father/mother and will speak first.

■ TO HELP YOU

a) In this task you need to explain to the Spanish family you are staying with why you are late home. Perhaps you missed the last bus home, or maybe you went to a café with some friends. It is likely that you'll need a verb in the preterite tense.

b) This is the unpredictable task! In the circumstances, what additional explanation or reason might the family want?

c) You can use the present tense for this since perhaps the reaction is always the same. Is it positive or is it negative? Maybe they get worried or angry, or they don't give you any more money to go out. Maybe it doesn't matter very much to them. Whatever the case you will probably need a verb in the third person plural.

d) After resolving this issue you now have to mention **two** activities that you're going to do tomorrow. Perhaps you can begin by using the near future with the verb *ir*, followed by infinitives. Keep them fairly straightforward, and don't worry too much about what time you'll get back home!

■ JOT DOWN YOUR ANSWERS

a) _____

b) _____

c) _____

d) _____

TEACHER'S ROLE

1 Introduce the situation and then ask the candidate why he/she is so late.
   Estás hablando con el padre/la madre de tu amigo español/tu amiga española. Yo soy el padre/la madre.
   ¿Por qué llegas tan tarde?

2 ! Allow the candidate to explain why he/she is so late.
   Ask the candidate why he/she did not telephone.
   ¿Por qué no llamaste por teléfono?

3 Allow the candidate to say why he/she did not telephone.
   Ask how his/her parents react if he/she arrives home late.
   Si llegas tarde a casa, ¿cómo reaccionan tus padres?

4 Allow the candidate to say how his/her parents react.
   Say it does not matter and ask what he/she is going to do tomorrow.
   Elicit **two** activities.
   No importa. ¿Qué vas a hacer mañana?

5 Allow the candidate to say **two** things he/she is going to do tomorrow.
   End the conversation by saying you hope he/she has a good time.
   Vale. Que lo pases bien.

■ MARK SCHEME

	0	1	2	3	4
	Message not communicated	Appropriate response/ difficulty or ambiguity/ some relevant information	Appropriate and unambiguous/minor errors or minor omissions	Appropriate and full response/minor errors cause no ambiguity/ TWO minor errors max.	Appropriate and correct response/task fully accomplished/NO SIGNIFICANT ERROR/ ONE minor error max.
a)		Ambiguity caused by inappropriate tense, e.g. *Voy a una cafetería con mis amigos.*	Appropriate reason **without** verb(s)	Appropriate reason **with** verb(s)	Appropriate reason for getting home late **with** verb(s), e.g. *Perdí el último autobús a casa.*
b)			Appropriate reason **without** verb(s) Inappropriate tense with no ambiguity, e.g. *No hay un teléfono.*	Appropriate reason **with** verb(s)	Appropriate reason for not telephoning home **with** verb(s), e.g. *No tenía dinero./No había teléfono.*
c)	Incorrect part of verb		Appropriate reaction **without** verb(s), e.g. *preocupados*	Appropriate reaction **with** verb(s)	Appropriate reaction **with** verb(s), e,g, *(Mis padres) se enfadan.* Present tense OK
d)		**One** activity only	Appropriate response **without** verb(s), e.g. *Tenis y película.*	**Two** activities **with** verb(s)	**Two** activities **with** verb(s), e.g. *(Mañana) (voy a) jugar al tenis y ver una película.* Infinitive or present tense OK

CANDIDATE'S ROLE

> Your Spanish friend is staying with you. You are really keen to go to a football match. Your friend has heard about problems involving football fans and is not sure.
>
> **a)** • *Tu sugerencia.*
> **b)** • *Tus **dos** razones.*
> **c)** • *Tu defensa de los fans y tu razón.*
> **d)** • ❗
>
> When you see ❗ you will have to respond to something which you have not prepared. Your teacher will play the part of your friend and will speak first.

■ TO HELP YOU

a) In this task you need to say that you want to go to a football match. To say 'I want ...' or 'I would like ...' use the verb *querer* (present tense, or special form of the conditional) or *gustar* (conditional tense). The second verb, 'to go', needs to be in the infinitive. Remember the little word for 'to' in Spanish, too!

b) You can use your imagination to suggest **two** reasons for going to the match. Perhaps it's an important match, or the atmosphere is great, or your team always scores goals, or they are the two best teams in the country, or something like that.

c) In this task you need to say something to defend football fans and give a reason. Perhaps they are responsible/important/lively/friendly, for example ... all because they help their team/love good football/have a good sense of humour, or something like that. Remember to use the third person plural of your verb(s).

d) This is the unpredictable task! Remember that your friend is not sure about going. Maybe he/she has another obstacle to put in the way, and maybe you can help!

■ JOT DOWN YOUR ANSWERS

a) _____

b) _____

c) _____

d) _____

TEACHER'S ROLE

1 Begin the conversation by setting the scene and asking the candidate what you can both do next week.
Estás en tu casa. Estás hablando con tu amigo español/tu amiga española. Yo soy tu amigo/amiga. ¿Qué hacemos la semana que viene?

2 Allow the candidate to say he/she wants to go to a football match.
Tell the candidate you are not sure. Ask why he/she wants to go. Elicit **two** reasons.
No estoy seguro/segura. ¿Por qué quieres ir?

3 Allow the candidate to give **two** reasons for wanting to go to the match.
Say you are still not sure as you have heard there are problems with fans at matches. Ask what the candidate thinks and elicit a reason.

No sé. Dicen que los fans son un problema. ¿Cuál es tu opinión? . . . ¿Por qué?

4 ❗ Allow the candidate to give an opinion with a reason.
Agree to go to the match, but say you have a problem – it is expensive and you do not have enough money. Ask what the candidate suggests to overcome the problem.
Muy bien, vamos. Pero tengo un problema. No tengo mucho dinero. ¿Qué puedo hacer?

5 Allow the candidate to suggest a solution.
End the conversation by agreeing with the candidate's solution.
¡Muy bien!

■ MARK SCHEME

	0	1	2	3	4
	Message not communicated	Appropriate response/ difficulty or ambiguity/ some relevant information	Appropriate and unambiguous/minor errors or minor omissions	Appropriate and full response/minor errors cause no ambiguity/ TWO minor errors max.	Appropriate and correct response/task fully accomplished/NO SIGNIFICANT ERROR/ ONE minor error max.
a)	Inappropriate response, e.g. *el fútbol* on its own	Response causing ambiguity, e.g. *Quiero un partido de fútbol.*	To say he/she wants to go to a football match **without** verb(s)	To say he/she wants to go to a football match **with** verb(s)	To say he/she wants to go to a football match **with** verb(s), e.g. *Quiero ir a un partido de fútbol.*
b)		**One** detail only	**Two** reasons **without** verb(s), e.g. *Equipo excelente y muchos goles.*	**Two** reasons **with** verb(s)	**Two** reasons for wanting to go to the match **with** verb(s), e.g. *Mi equipo siempre gana y el ambiente es estupendo.*
c)		Defence of fans but no reason	Defence of fans and reason **without** verb(s)	Defence of fans and reason **with** verb(s)	Defence of fans and reason **with** verb(s), e.g. *Son responsables (porque) quieren mucho a su club.*
d)			Appropriate response **without** verb(s) *No es caro.*	Appropriate response **with** verb(s)	Appropriate response **with** verb(s), e.g. *Mi padre compra las entradas./(Yo) tengo suficiente dinero.*

VOCABULARY

A

it's about   *trata de ...*

abroad   *(al) extranjero*

accident   *accidente* (m)

accommodation   *alojamiento* (m)

actor   *actor* (m)

advertisement   *anuncio* (m)

already   *ya* (adv)

angry   *enfadado* (adj)

ankle   *tobillo* (m)

to answer   *contestar* (vb)

arm   *brazo* (m)

to arrive   *llegar* (vb)

at   *a* (prep)

atmosphere   *ambiente* (m)

B

back, at the ~   *al fondo*

bad   *malo* (adj)

bag   *bolsa* (f), *bolso* (m)

to be (+ location)   *estar* (vb)

to be (+ permanent characteristic)   *ser* (vb)

to be (+ profession)   *ser* (vb)

to be (+ temporary characteristic)   *estar* (vb)

to be (+ weather)   *hacer* (vb); *estar* (vb)

to be back (return)   *volver* (vb)

because   *porque*

to become   *hacerse* (vb)

beside   *al lado de* (prep)

to book   *reservar* (vb)

boring   *aburrido* (adj)

boss   *jefe* (m), *jefa* (f)

to break   *romper(se)* (vb)

bullfight   *corrida* (f) *de toros*

to buy   *comprar* (vb)

by, near   *al lado de* (prep); *cerca de* (prep)

by (+ transport)   *en* (prep)

C

café   *cafeteria* (f)

can, be able   *poder* (vb)

car   *coche* (m)

centre   *centro* (m)

to change   *cambiar* (vb)

cinema   *cine* (m)

class   *clase* (f)

climate   *clima* (m)

club   *club* (m)

coach   *autocar* (m)

colleague   *colega* (m)

college   *colegio* (m)

colour   *color* (m)

to come   *venir* (vb)

to complain   *quejarse* (vb)

cost   *precio* (m)

cost of living   *coste* (m) *de la vida*

to cut   *cortar(se)* (vb)

D

dangerous   *peligroso* (adj)

dessert   *postre* (m)

dirty   *sucio* (adj)

disco   *discoteca* (f)

discount   *descuento* (m)

drink   *bebida* (f)

to drink   *beber* (vb)

during   *durante* (adv)

E

to earn   *ganar* (vb)

easy   *fácil* (adj)

to eat   *comer* (vb)

enough   *bastante* (adj), *suficiente* (adj)

entrance   *entrada* (f)

evening   *tarde* (f)

exams   *exámenes* (mpl)

excellent   *estupendo* (adj), *fenomenal* (adj)

exciting   *emocionante* (adj)

excursion   *excursión* (f)

expensive   *caro* (adj)

experience   *experiencia* (f)

F

to fall   *caer(se)* (vb)

family   *familia* (f)

fantastic   *estupendo* (adj)

fast   *rápido* (adj)

to feel   *sentirse* (vb)

film   *película* (f)

to find   *encontrar* (vb)

to finish   *terminar* (vb)

first   *primero* (adj)

flight   *vuelo* (m)

food   *comida* (f)

football   *fútbol* (m)

for (+ length of time)   *desde hace*

to forget   *olvidar* (vb)
free time   *tiempo libre*
free, at no cost   *gratis* (adv)
free, available   *libre* (adj)
friend   *amigo* (m); *amiga* (f)
friendly   *amable, amistoso* (adj)
from   *de* (prep)
from … until …   *desde … hasta …*
fun   *divertido* (adj)

G

to get, become   *hacerse* (vb)
to get, catch (a train)   *coger* (vb); *tomar* (vb)
to get, find (e.g. a job)   *encontrar* (vb)
to get, receive   *recibir* (vb)
to go   *ir* (vb)
to go out   *salir* (vb) *(de …)*
good   *bueno* (adj)
ground   *suelo* (m)
guide   *guía* (m) (f)

H

hand   *mano* (f)
happy   *contento* (adj)
to have (+ past participle)   *haber* (vb)
to have (own)   *tener* (vb)
to have (take, eat)   *tomar* (vb)
to have to   *tener* (vb) *que*
health   *salud* (f)
to help   *ayudar* (vb)
hole   *agujero* (m)
holidays   *vacaciones* (fpl)
home   *casa* (f)
homework   *deberes* (mpl)
hours (of work)   *horas* (fpl) *de trabajo*
hungry, to be ~   *tener* (vb) *hambre* (m)
to hurt   *hacerse* (vb) *daño en*

I

immediately   *inmediatamente* (adj)
important   *importante* (adj)
interesting   *interesante* (adj)

J

jumper   *jersey* (m)

K

kind   *simpático* (adj)
knee   *rodilla* (f)

L

last   *último* (adj)
to last   *durar* (vb)
late   *tarde*
lazy   *perezoso* (adj)
to leave   *dejar* (vb), *salir* (vb) *(de …)*
leg   *pierna* (f)
let's …   *vamos a …*

to listen (to)   *escuchar* (vb)
lively   *animado* (adj), *activo* (adj)
long   *largo* (adj)
long, how ~?   *¿cuánto tiempo?*
a lot of (many)   *mucho* (adj)
lots of (much)   *mucho* (adj)
to love, like a lot   *encantar* (vb)
lunch, to have ~   *comer* (vb)

M

to make   *hacer* (vb)
match (e.g. football)   *partido* (m)
to matter   *importar* (vb)
to meet   *encontrar* (vb)
to miss (e.g. a bus)   *perder* (vb)
money   *dinero* (m)
money back   *reembolso* (m)
month   *mes* (m)
music   *música* (f)
must, have to   *tener* (vb) *que*

N

near   *cerca de* (prep)
necessary   *necesario* (adj)
next   *próximo* (adj)
next (beside)   *… de al lado* (adv)
by night   *por la noche*
noise   *ruido* (m)
noisy   *ruidoso* (adj)
number   *número* (m)

O

on   *en* (prep)
on (with day, date)   *el*
other   *otro* (adj)

P

to pay   *pagar* (vb)
people   *personas* (fpl), *gente* (f)
people, young ~   *jóvenes* (mpl)
place, site (in campsite)   *parcela* (f)
to plan (to do)   *tener* (vb) *la intención de …*
to play   *jugar* (vb) *a …*
police station   *comisaría* (f)
problem   *problema* (m)

Q

question   *pregunta* (f)
quiet   *callado* (adj)

R

to read   *leer* (vb)
really, very much   *mucho* (adv)
to receive   *recibir* (vb)
reduction   *reducción* (f)
refund   *reembolso* (m)
region   *región* (f)
responsible   *responsable* (adj)

© John Murray

to return   *volver* (vb)
rubbish   *basura* (f)
rubbish bin   *cubo* (m) *de basura*
rules   *reglas* (fpl)

S

salary   *salario* (m)
on Saturday   *el sábado*
seat   *asiento* (m)
second   *segundo* (adj)
to see   *ver* (vb)
to send   *mandar* (vb)
sense of humour   *sentido* (m) *del humor*
to serve   *servir* (vb)
shade, in the ~   *a la sombra*
shopping, to go ~   *ir* (vb) *de compras*
to show, indicate   *mostrar* (vb)
to show, put on   *poner* (vb)
sick, to feel ~   *tener* (vb) *náuseas* (fpl)
to ski   *esquiar* (vb)
skiing   *esquí* (m)
slowly   *lentamente* (adv)
small   *pequeño* (adj)
to smoke   *fumar* (vb)
smoke   *humo* (m)
soap opera   *telenovela* (f)
to speak   *hablar* (vb)
to spend (money)   *gastar* (vb)
to spend (time)   *pasar* (vb)
sport   *deporte* (m)
sports centre   *polideportivo* (m)
stairs   *escalera* (f)
to start   *empezar* (vb)
story   *historia* (f)
straightaway   *en seguida, ahora mismo* (adj)
street   *calle* (f)
strict   *estricto* (adj), *severo* (adj)
to study   *estudiar* (vb)
stupid   *estúpido* (adj)
subject (school)   *asignatura* (f)
suitcase   *maleta* (f)
summer   *verano* (m)
sun, in the ~   *al sol*

T

table   *mesa* (f)
team   *equipo* (m)
to telephone   *llamar* (vb) *por teléfono* (m)

television   *televisión* (f)
tent   *tienda* (m)
things to do   *actividades* (fpl), *cosas* (fpl) *que hacer*
this morning   *esta mañana* (adv)
to throw   *tirar* (vb)
ticket (for show)   *entrada* (f)
tight   *ajustado* (adj)
time, to have ~   *tener* (vb) *tiempo* (m)
timetable   *horario* (m)
tired   *cansado* (adj)
to   *a* (prep)
too   *demasiado* (adv)
to travel   *viajar* (vb)
traveller's cheques   *cheques* (mpl) *de viajero*
to twist   *torcer(se)* (vb)

U

uniform   *uniforme* (m)
university   *universidad* (f)
unwell   *enfermo* (adj)

V

very   *muy* (adv)
to visit   *visitar* (vb)

W

waiter   *camarero* (m)
to want   *querer* (vb)
to watch   *ver* (vb)
to wear   *llevar* (vb)
weather   *tiempo* (m) (see 'to be')
weekend   *fin* (m) *de semana*
work   *trabajo* (m)
to work (earn a living)   *trabajar* (vb)
to work (operate)   *funcionar* (vb)
work experience   *prácticas* (fpl) *laborales; experiencia*
   (f) *laboral*
worried   *preocupado* (adj)

Y

yesterday   *ayer* (adv)
young   *joven* (adj)